Communicating around Interculturality in Research and Education

This book does not instruct the reader how to communicate interculturally but supports them in reflecting on how they can (re-)negotiate and (re-)construct knowledge(s), ideologies and relations around the notion of interculturality.

Anchored in the author's original and thought-provoking perspectives on interculturality, this interdisciplinary and global-minded book explores how communicating around the notion cannot do away with ideologisms, issues of language and translation or the problematization of voice and silence in research and education. Written in an original and stimulating way, relying on different writing genres and styles to 'mimic' the dynamism and flexibility of the very notion under review, the author urges us to (un-)voice, scrutinize, nurture and galvanize our ways of dealing with interculturality alone and together with others in academia. The very specific focus of the book, communicating around interculturality (instead of 'doing' interculturality), represents a fresh and important move for observing, analyzing, speaking of and contributing to today's complex and divided world.

The title is aimed at researchers, students and educators interested in examining and enriching their own takes on interculturality, from a more reflexive and interactive perspective.

Fred Dervin is Professor of Multicultural Education at the University of Helsinki, Finland. Prof. Dervin specializes in intercultural communication education, the sociology of multiculturalism and international mobilities in education. Exploring the politics of interculturality within and beyond the 'canon' of intercultural communication education research has been one of Dervin's idée fixes in his work over the past 20 years. He has published over 160 articles and 80 books in different languages on identity, interculturality and mobility/migration. His latest books published with Routledge also include *The Paradoxes of Interculturality* and *Intercultural Communication Education and Research* (co-authored with R'boul).

New Perspectives on Teaching Interculturality
Series Editors:
Fred Dervin
Professor of multicultural education at the University of Helsinki.

About the Series

This book series publishes original and innovative single-authored and edited volumes contributing robust, new and genuinely global studies to the exciting field of research and practice of interculturality in education. The series aims to enrich the current objectives of 'doing' and teaching interculturality in the 21st century by problematizing Euro- and Western-centric perspectives and giving a voice to other original and under-explored approaches. The series promotes the search for different epistemologies, cutting-edge interdisciplinarity and the importance of reflexive and critical translation in teaching about this important notion. Finally, *New Perspectives on Teaching Interculturality* serves as a platform for dialogue amongst the global community of educators, researchers, and students.

Teaching Interculturality 'Otherwise'
Edited by Fred Dervin, Mei Yuan and Sude

The Paradoxes of Interculturality
A Toolbox of Out-of-the-box Ideas for Intercultural Communication Education
Fred Dervin

Intercultural Communication Education and Research
Reenvisioning Fundamental Notions
Hamza R'boul, Fred Dervin

Communicating around Interculturality in Research and Education
Fred Dervin

For a full list of titles in this series, visit www.routledge.com/New-Perspectives-on-Teaching-Interculturality/book-series/NPTI

Communicating around Interculturality in Research and Education

Fred Dervin

LONDON AND NEW YORK

First published in 2024
by Routledge
4 Park Square, Milton Park, Abingdon, Oxon OX14 4RN

and by Routledge
605 Third Avenue, New York, NY 10158

Routledge is an imprint of the Taylor & Francis Group, an informa business

© 2024 Fred Dervin

The right of Fred Dervin to be identified as author of this work has been asserted in accordance with sections 77 and 78 of the Copyright, Designs and Patents Act 1988.

All rights reserved. No part of this book may be reprinted or reproduced or utilised in any form or by any electronic, mechanical, or other means, now known or hereafter invented, including photocopying and recording, or in any information storage or retrieval system, without permission in writing from the publishers.

Trademark notice: Product or corporate names may be trademarks or registered trademarks, and are used only for identification and explanation without intent to infringe.

British Library Cataloguing-in-Publication Data
A catalogue record for this book is available from the British Library

Library of Congress Cataloging-in-Publication Data
Names: Dervin, Fred, 1974– author.
Title: Communicating around interculturality in research and education / Fred Dervin.
Description: Abingdon, Oxon ; New York, NY : Routledge, 2024. | Series: New perspectives on teaching interculturality | Includes bibliographical references and index.
Identifiers: LCCN 2023022048 (print) | LCCN 2023022049 (ebook) | ISBN 9781032588599 (hardback) | ISBN 9781032588773 (paperback) | ISBN 9781003451938 (ebook)
Subjects: LCSH: Intercultural communication in education. | Interdisciplinary research. | Intercultural communication. | Multiculturalism.
Classification: LCC LC1099 .D4667 2024 (print) | LCC LC1099 (ebook) | DDC 370.117—dc23/eng/20230512
LC record available at https://lccn.loc.gov/2023022048
LC ebook record available at https://lccn.loc.gov/2023022049

ISBN: 978-1-032-58859-9 (hbk)
ISBN: 978-1-032-58877-3 (pbk)
ISBN: 978-1-003-45193-8 (ebk)

DOI: 10.4324/9781003451938

Typeset in Times New Roman
by Apex CoVantage, LLC

Contents

List of Figures and tables vi
Acknowledgments vii

1 Interculturality is dead; long live interculturality! 1

2 (Un-)voicing 15

3 Scrutinizing 36

4 Nurturing and galvanizing 66

5 Communicating as a lesson in humility 84

Index *90*

Figures and tables

Figures

Figure 2.1　The multivoicedness of an ancient Chinese book　　19
Figure 3.1　Sign at a café in China containing the
　　　　　　 characters for *civility/civilization/civilized* and *courtesy*　56

Tables

Table 3.1　Publications focusing on issues of translation
　　　　　　 for interculturality　　61

Acknowledgments

I would like to thank Publisher Lian Sun and her team for their continued support and professionalism.

While I was writing this book, I often interacted with Hamza R'boul, who has become an important 'ally' and friend in deconstructing the notion of interculturality. Thanks are due to my Ph.D. researchers for stimulating my thinking during our seminars and informal discussions. Many of the points made about communicating around interculturality in this book were inspired by our dialogues.

This book is dedicated to Leena-Mummo, the 'midwife' of my obsession with interculturality.

1 Interculturality is dead; long live interculturality!

[Vocalizing]

1. Why would I want to publish a book on communicating around interculturality *in research and education*, claiming that it is an urgent aspect of scholarship on the notion?
2. Is the difference between *communication around interculturality* and *interculturality as a communicative phenomenon* clear to you? How much do you think that these two overlap? In the book, I will be creating what might appear to be an artificial boundary between them.
3. What 'burning issues' about communicating around interculturality would you want to see addressed in this book? What are you expecting to learn about it?

Conducting as an entry into the book topic

Since my early twenties, alongside my interest in interculturality, I have been fascinated by the role of the music conductor who has to coordinate and communicate with orchestras, choruses, and musical ensembles, pacing and stressing the rhythmic beat in order for them to perform in synergy. A conductor ensures (amongst others) order and technical mastery (e.g., cues, dynamics, expression) while providing artistic and theoretical knowledge to orchestras. I have observed and examined hundreds of conductors around the world and in videos – their charisma, use of arms, hand gestures, batons, and other means to guide players and singers, often following a score. I have wondered at the ways they manage (or not manage) to unite the efforts of musicians, using (mostly but not only) nonverbal means. I have also always been stunned by the fact that a conductor must be in two places at the same time somehow: the real time of the performance as well as ahead of time, keeping an eye ahead in the score sections. Amongst some of my favourite conductors are Leonard Bernstein (U.S.), Pierre Boulez (France/Germany) and Susanna Mälkki (Finland). The very word conductor comes from Latin for "a carrier" and "to lead or bring together, contribute, serve" (*together, with + to lead*).

DOI: 10.4324/9781003451938-1

Watching performances, I am fascinated by conductors' different styles, personalities and ways of engaging with members of an orchestra, and the complexities they have to deal with during rehearsals and concerts, which could make conducting one of the most difficult 'communicative' jobs. Boulez (1986) explains that one conductor might appear to be slow and noble but very efficient, another might be curbing gestures or be an intro- or extra-vert. Every time they play with a different orchestra, the musicians have to adapt to the conductor and the conductor to the orchestra, negotiating through gestures and music the content of the sounds produced together. When asked how to become a good conductor, Boulez (1986) often argued that there is no miraculous recipe and that one needs to find an answer to this question by oneself. Many Finnish conductors were trained by Jorma Panula, who supported each of them in developing their own style of conducting, e.g., communicating through hands and eyes, without speaking – the score only can speak (Franck, 2022)! One of his former students and now world-class conductor Mikko Franck (2022) explains:

> Panula's pedagogy is very concrete. He talks about the fundamentals. What is the role of the conductor? It's all about helping musicians play and interpret music. So, you need a precise technique. From the beginning, he told me to abandon all mannerisms, any superfluous gesture. Each gesture must be useful to the musician. The basic principle is: if you can't help them, at least try not to disturb them too much. . . . Everything can be summed up in the clarity of the technique of the hands and gestures. The communication of intentions must be crystal clear.[1]

Franck (2022) adds that the main difference between, e.g., learning to play the piano and conducting is that, for the piano, the technique (learnt from/with others) is vital, while for conducting, the technique comes from inside – one's own identity and even one's physical appearance.

The more I read and reflect on conducting, the more I think that what we educators, scholars, intellectuals and also students who work on interculturality is of a very similar nature. This book focuses on the very specific topic of communicating around interculturality as 'professional' interculturalists. In this book, I argue that there is no technique to communicate around interculturality with the 'world' and that, like conductors with an orchestra, we need to develop our own techniques, reflecting on what communicating could mean and entail with different kinds of interlocutors (other educators/scholars, students, decision-makers, the general public, etc.).

Communicating *around* . . .

> "The single biggest problem in communication is the illusion that it has taken place".
>
> Shaw (quoted by Bibby, 2017, p. 71)

The last three years have been rather painful to observe and analyse for interculturalists. The world is currently very much divided and polarized – which is very much reminiscent of similar divisions from the past, like the Cold War at the end of the 20th century. The repeated social, economic, political, and ideological crises since early 2020 have been the sources of misinformation, misunderstandings, non-understandings and clashes between different parts of the world, which makes trying to promote any kind of dialogue around *who we are, what we do* and *try to say*, alone and together with others, a real challenge. Many doors are closing from the so-called 'West', while, at the same time, many other parts of the world are retracting inside bubbles they are creating for themselves or are pushed to create through others' alienation and discrimination. Bridging these separate spaces is what should preoccupy us as scholars, educators and people who care about the world today and tomorrow. Since spring 2020, I have published over 40 books and articles by myself and with scholars from Europe and China, reflecting on what is happening to us and proposing new ways of dealing with this 'new world'. Each of these publications represents a handmade brick for building a house that will never be ready, considering the complexities of the task. The COVID-19 pandemic has opened my eyes to many of the problems that we are facing with this giant mountain called interculturality. And, although calls for dialogue and tolerance are still very much with us after the pandemic (I am thinking here of the tired 2023 campaign about the Chinese language, 中文:增进文明对话, *Facilitating Dialogues across Civilizations*), communicating interculturally appears to be very much in trouble today.

There is another dimension of interculturality which I believe deserves our attention since it could affect what we 'do' together interculturally more than one might think: *communicating around interculturality in research and education*. As much as interculturality seems to be divided in everyday life and in political and (social) media discourses, the notion in academia and education also shows signs of division, exhaustion and injustice. While Europe seems to focus on ideological entries such as democracy and non-essentialism, China calls for cultural confidence and building up a community of shared future. While these values might overlap in terms of content and concrete outcomes, the way they are constructed and spoken of in research and education may not contribute to communicating smoothly and convincingly in English as a global language and other languages. At least two recent books seem to have identified some of these issues, problematized them and offered (some) solutions: *The Politics of Researching Multilingually* (Holmes et al., 2022) and *Methodological Issues and Challenges in Researching Transculturally* (Victoria, 2022). I note, however, that they do not address upfront interculturality as an object of research and education that global scholars, students and educators construct and attempt to negotiate around the world.

Let me share a few vignettes illustrating the issue of communicating around interculturality.[2]

[Reviewing recent literature published in Mainland China on interculturality with my colleague Ning Chen – and its companions such as multicultural, culturally responsive but also Minzu, a notion used in China which refers to so-called Chinese 'minority' education (see Dervin & Yuan, 2021; Wang, 2022) – I note the following problems when working between Chinese and English: 1. The word Minzu is misused to refer to the American context of multicultural education. An article entitled 美国智库民族教育政策研究的差异性公平观建构 – 以教育信托为例 (which translates as *The Construction of Differentiated Equity Concept in the Study of Minority (Minzu) Education Policy in the United States: A Case Study of Education Trust*), uses the Chinese expression 民族 (Minzu) in Chinese to refer to U.S. Minority education policies. The very word Minzu in Chinese is 'hyper-specific' to the Chinese context (it refers to the 56 official groups of people whose 'cultures' and 'languages' can differ immensely in the Middle Kingdom). This misuse will undoubtedly lead to mis- or even non-communication between different scholars, educators and students across China and the U.S., if they get to communicate with each other around the content of this publication. 2. We searched for 'culturally responsive' (a very popular ideological construct from the U.S., see Snyder & Fenner, 2021) in a Chinese database, using the Chinese equivalent of 文化回应, and found out that most of the publications returned by the system are mostly publications from the U.S. in English, with very few in Chinese using this important (and yet problematically dominating) label.]

[In preparing this book, I was very lucky to be able to interact indirectly with reviewers who provided some good feedback about what I was trying to say and do with it. I noted that some of their comments and suggestions were indicative of what I want to address with the book. For example, one reviewer wrote: "The book is interdisciplinary, or rather, transdisciplinary and transnational. It will appeal to interculturalists worldwide". Reading the comment and stopping on every single word in the sentences, I wonder what all these words mean and if I understand them the same way (as much as you, my readers, might (not) be confused by them): *interdisciplinary, transdisciplinary, transnational*. The different roots of these adjectives (inter- and trans-) are very polysemic in English and in other languages, while they may not even have equivalents in other languages.

About the first draft of this introduction, another reviewer was of the following opinion:

Although I fully appreciate the author's (or authors') intention to be self-reflexive throughout the book, I think the first two pages of the Introduction contain too many personal and minor details. They also contain observations placed in squared brackets, which are distractive. Also, I think that the reference to the 'famous white man' is patronizing somehow, even if, of course, it was meant to be highly ironic.

There are many interesting points here that show potential problems of mis-/non-communication between the reviewer and myself. Their take (*personal opinions – see 'too many personal and minor details'*) on my style of writing, tone, honesty and word use shows that we share different views on the way(s) scholarship on interculturality could/should be written and the place and positioning of the researcher in their own writing. These are, of course, *opinions* based on different ideological views (note: they do not claim to be 'scientific') that need to be respected, and I am thankful for such observations since they help me see how people can perceive my current production.

One final example from the reviews has to do with what I now call the obsession to 'define' the problematically definable . . . A reviewer noted:

> Since there are circulating very different understandings of the concepts of 'interculturality'/'intercultural communication'/'culture', but also of 'language(s)', it would be helpful if you could briefly state in the introduction how you are using these terms – especially as this has also implications for how you are conceptualizing the role of language and of translations (. . . that you are not aiming at 'translating cultures' for instance).

I have explained elsewhere that I do understand this (somewhat tired) obsession, having myself, over the years prior to the pandemic, done this work in very restrictive and imposing ways (Dervin, 2016). However, today, having worked and discussed with hundreds of scholars, educators, and students from around the world, I do realize that my role is not to define – in other words, impose – a limited and limiting view on what such a complex notion of interculturality is, should be and entail. Writing from a very small corner of the world (Finland, European Union), influenced by dominating and limited ideologies, experiences and relationships, I experience, like all social beings, contradictions and inconsistencies in the way I think about and operationalize interculturality as an individual, a scholar and an educator. Faced with the extreme complexities of what interculturality could mean and entail, I cannot spell out my convictions about the notion, somehow pretending to do it in a 'scientific' way, to influence readers, students and colleagues located anywhere on this big planet who have their own ways of engaging with other people and institutions *interculturally*. Although this influence is occurring all the time (some scholars in Mainland China make use of the hyper-European framework of Democratic Culture to teach interculturality; some teacher educators in Finland 'import' the U.S. ideologies of culturally responsive teaching and anti-racism in a country where such positions are not even spoken of in terms that allow engaging seriously with them), with this book, I want to reflect with you on how we could communicate around interculturality together in fairer, more balanced and open-minded ways, beyond solid definitions, frameworks and models, reconsidering ideological takes and words we use to engage with the notion. *In other words: Communication as a mirror of communication.*]

[Conversing with students and colleagues from China in English as a global academic language, I hear the following phrases: 'University capacity', 'intercultural quality teachers', 'the need to promote the excellent traditional culture for Minzu', 'we need to tell Chinese stories well' and 'students should cultivate cross-cultural intelligence'. I am aware that some of these are direct translations from Chinese. I also realize that these phrases are derived from the 'Chinese' ideological milieu, which makes it very difficult to grasp, negotiate and work with if we don't spend quality time trying to unpack them together. I am speaking to them, I feel I understand them, but I realize that we are 'floating past each other'. I also use words that they do not necessarily position the same way and vice versa.]

[I just finished reviewing a paper for an international journal, which contains many assertions I do not understand, although they could appear as 'obvious' and 'easy' to some of us. One such sentence says: "Teachers need to understand and respect different cultures in their classroom". Throughout my 25-year career, I must have read this sentence a thousand times in the different languages that I can understand. I am convinced that I must have uttered something similar in the past. However, like the other vignettes, I see every word *individually* and I think I understand what they each might mean (maybe). Put together, I am easily confused. What does *understanding different cultures* mean? How about *respecting* them? And especially for 'teachers' in different parts of the world, with different ideological and economic-political pressure?]

Look at the state of the world in spring 2023: *interculturality is failing us*. What if the reasons for this failure are not because we haven't learnt each other's culture, become non-essentialists or adopted polysemic (and politically-manipulated) ideologies such as *tolerance* and *respect*, but because we haven't been concentrating enough on how to communicate around the notion in ways that have allowed us to change together, to re-consider the notion under newly negotiated perspectives or to adapt new forms of discourse around the notion that reflect criticality (of criticality), reflexivity and humility? I want us to consider seriously the assumption that concrete, everyday intercultural problems might be drawn directly from the way(s) we communicate around it in research and education.

[One could pastiche the saying 'The King is Dead, long live the King!' (a new King replaces a King when the latter has passed away) with 'Interculturality is dead; long live interculturality!'. Interculturality as an object of research and education – a meta-interculturality – versus interculturality as daily encounters.]

As we can see in the vignettes above, language is central in considering how, what, with whom and why we communicate in certain ways. Language in this book is considered (randomly): both a friend and a foe; a treasure to cherish; a mystery to be (partly) solved; a friendly, tolerant/tolerable gesture to the other; an act of possession; noise; silence; a pain soother; a violent weapon; an important part of our (changing) identity; 'divorce' from the complex realities of the world, which language can never help us grasp or express. None of these characteristics/dichotomies are meant to represent negative views on what language could be and does but stimulate aspects of a 'struggle' that we all have to face. Today, 'languaging' is constant in our neoliberal worlds, where one is urged to communicate as often as one can, even when one has nothing to say. In this constant flow and flood of words, communicating around interculturality in research and education represents an important objective, which could help shift and push self and others to other spaces of co-creation.

A multidimensionally *intercultural* book about *interculturality*

Communication in this book refers to ways of engaging with others in academia and education: reading, listening, speaking, writing, interacting, in one or different languages, in direct and/or mediated ways. Communicating must also be considered under the lens of the different genres in which it is embedded (on academic genres, see: Berkenkotter et al., 2012):

Writing: articles, chapters, abstracts, books, reviews, evaluations, reports, (which can be descriptive, analytical, persuasive, reflexive and/or critical . . .)
Speaking: debates, lectures, defenses, interviews, symposia, invited keynotes . . .

I hypothesize that, in every corner of the world, every day, some scholars, teachers, decision-makers, students and (why not?) parents talk about interculturality or any of its companion terms (multi-, trans-, cross-cultural, global . . .). In that sense, we are all producers, consumers and promoters but also destroyers, negators and silencers of discourses of interculturality. We communicate, mis-communicate and non-communicate – and often with all these occurring at the same time. We create monologues, dialogues and pseudo-dialogues but also short-circuit our conversations. If I think about my daily life as a scholar, intellectual and educator, I:

Address different kinds of (small and large) audiences;
Analyse;
Challenge;
Convince;
Criticize (my own criticality);
Define;
Dis-/agree;
Distract (from the truth?);

Explain;
Listen;
Question;
Read;
Rework/modify;
Silence;
Translate multilingually;
... (often without realizing).

Looking at the titles of research articles published in international journals in 2021–2022, I note that the authors communicate around the following verbs found in the titles of their articles:

[Bridging across... Capturing... Constructing... Decentring... Decolonizing... Developing... Engineering... Expanding... Exploring... Integrating... Liberating... Making sense of... Negotiating... Problematizing... Questioning... Reimagining... Revisiting... Searching for... Shifting perspectives... Transcending... Transforming...]

Writing this book could be considered a (liberating – compared to a research article of 7,000 words) complex act of interculturality (but isn't interculturality always complex?) since I am not sure who will be reading this book concretely, or if they are going to understand what I am saying and trying to argue for the way(s) I do. I know that we could have a lot of ideas, positions and ways of discoursing interculturality in common. I am also aware that we could misunderstand each other in the different languages we could use to communicate with each other, (maybe) being unaware of the different connotations that a given word might have in English and other languages. [Communication is far too complex for us to know if we are really communicating with each other. Sometimes we might be 'good' at it, at other times, we fail]. I also know that I will probably only get to meet a very small proportion of my readers and continue the discussions from the next chapters together. Writing the book also means communicating with myself (in other words: looking at myself communicating around interculturality *with* and *in* different voices), different kinds of knowledge from research, education, the arts, philosophy (amongst others), different ways of expressing and constructing different objects in different languages, a multitude of (past and present) experiences of interculturality, 'real' and 'imagined' encounters...

The book goes beyond some kind of 'cannibal' approach whereby I tell/order you, my readers, how you *should* communicate. I want to run away from this violent approach, which is often practiced in academia – and which I have 'done' myself. Instead, I note what we could/should bear in mind, observe and discuss in the process of changing together and balancing each other in the ways we communicate around interculturality.

Since interculturality is in us all and thus cannot be separated from our identity as scholars, educators, and students, I do not shy away from putting my own subjectivities on the table. Too many publications on interculturality 'pretend' to be outside of the sphere of the intercultural encounters and experiences that they describe, problematize and analyze, as if they were exterior to them. However, whenever I interview someone for research or observe a class, my own presence cannot but be part of the acts of interculturality taking place. 'Merely' asking someone how they define interculturality already opens a Pandora's box of terms, ideologies and stereotypes that need to be reconsidered *again and again*.

I don't like to define interculturality (as a phenomenon) anymore or to tell people what they should do about it. I used to do that, and I have written extensively over the past years to explain why I am not too eager to do it today. My reasons include my fear of indoctrinating and silencing alternative, less powerful voices and also my wish to restrain my own influence in a world that needs to listen to anyone located in different parts of the world – not just from my own 'corner' of the world. To get rid of the issue of defining interculturality now, let me share a few thoughts about where I stand in relation to the notion today. For me, interculturality is a never-ending process of encounters between people of different origins, nationalities and languages (amongst others), whose ideological worlds, mediated through complex languages, need to be renegotiated to cross over to each other when they meet. Interculturality is thus not about '*cultures meeting*' (the concept of *culture* is too broad and, at times, empty to help us scholars and educators, see Piller, 2010) but about individuals whose visions of self, other and the world need to be spelt out *honestly, critically* and *modestly* so that they can start talking to each other. As such, no one can be 'perfect' at doing interculturality since it is always renegotiated and re-problematized when we meet as *individuals*. Interculturality is a lifelong process for which no one can ever be ready and for which no miraculous recipe can be applied. Interculturality is as complex, unpredictable and uncontrollable as *humanity* and *sociality* themselves. Interculturality always occurs within economic-political silos, which affect the ways we interact with each other, constructing who we have been made to believe we are. So, I repeat: *there is no easy and miraculous solution to 'good' or 'effective' interculturality*. Interculturality is something that we need to 'do' and 're-do' again and again. We can only communicate imperfectly around interculturality and try again without any success in sight.

Working with the book

This book won't teach you how to '*do*' interculturality as individuals, scholars, educators and students. This 'nice' and 'well-intentioned' goal appears outdated from the outset. As soon as I teach others how to engage interculturally, I cannot but put forward one set of ideologies that too easily turns into brainwashing and indoctrination.

This book is not about *intercultural communication*, but about how to communicate around the broader notion of interculturality in education and research – whereby individuals engage with people, ideas, ideologies, knowledges and subjectivities from another context. The book will not teach you how to communicate *properly* in these contexts, but support you in un-re-thinking communication as interculturalists. As such, the book tells us that we are both good and bad communicators; that communication is both possible and impossible while reminding us that human communication is a very hard job that no 'trick' can make invulnerable. The book describes what we all do willy-nilly when dealing with interculturality, i.e., we navigate between multifarious ideologies, recycle bits and pieces of information about the notion, ask questions about it and provide (often) unsatisfactory answers. Interculturality is a good example of the impossibility of expressing and grappling with the complexities of our social/human conditions.

Here are some of the questions that are addressed in-/directly in the book. I suggest that you often come back to them while reading the next chapters:

What does communicating around interculturality mean in different contexts?
Can we communicate around interculturality in English and other languages?
[Is it even possible to communicate around this polysemic and complex notion and its companions (multicultural, cross-cultural, global . . .)?]
Should we (try to) communicate around interculturality, especially with those we dis-/agree with and/or consider problematic to communicate with?
Who should be part of our acts of communication? In what language(s)?
What if I don't have anything to communicate around the notion? Should I be forced to communicate further around interculturality? By whom?
Why do we need to communicate?
How could we create a new (common and constantly renegotiable) language to communicate with each other around interculturality?
Should silence in research and education related to interculturality be promoted?
Finally, should dominating ideological voices be silenced to allow for more communication to happen? For example, what forms of silence should be disrupted?

In general, the book provides some discussions of the following questions: How ought we to talk to each other in complicated times like ours? How should we communicate around *interculturality*? How can we create spaces of interaction so that we can sit and listen to each other, creating together a sense of 'just' in-betweenness? Should we speak about interculturality to each other in our own languages and/or in a global language like English?

This book is meant for both novice and confirmed researchers and educators. It is not meant to serve as a textbook for communicating around interculturality and should be considered as an 'anti-manual' since it asks more questions than provides answers. [An anti-manual of communication]. It is written in special ways, which some readers may find somehow surprising. Since communicating around interculturality is unstable, uncertain and full of surprises, negotiations and changes, I have adopted a style of writing which reflects these characteristics. Each chapter contains different genres (e.g., short fragments, commentaries, excerpts from my notes and interactions with others) to force us to navigate between different ways of communicating beyond the illusionary unidirectionality of some academic texts. *Interculturality is never easy. It pleases while disappointing. It hurts while befriending. It beautifies while attacking. It lies while comforting. It manipulates while helping* . . . Communicating around it in research and education must move beyond the 'happy-go-lucky' of (rational and objectivizing) academic writing. Over the past years, I have argued for new approaches to writing about interculturality to force us out of our (aesthetic, academic and epistemic) comfort zones and protective bubbles (Dervin, 2022, 2023). As much as there is no 'magic recipe' to intercultural 'problems' (whatever this might mean), there is no 'magic solution' to communicating around them. My writing is meant to reflect these necessary struggles. The chapters discuss and present certain issues which you are free to explore, test, adopt, share and/or reject. The content of the chapters is all yours. Do as you wish.

This book was also written and constructed with reflexivity and criticality in mind – two central aspects of intercultural research and education. In order to reflect further on the questions, assertions and proposals made in the book, I include *[Vocalizing]* and *[Reflexive and Critical Potpourri]^5* sections systematically at the beginning and end of each chapter for the reader to continue their journey towards integrating reflections on communicating around interculturality into their daily work. A list of three interesting publications in English is also included at the end of Chapters 2, 3 and 4. Communicating around the notion is like breathing for interculturalists, and I am hoping to infuse new fresh air into a field that needs to face, increasingly, its own contradictions, (at times) misrepresentations and (genuinely) global complexities. Critical and reflexive communication about interculturality offers a solid platform for (real) inclusion, (real) cooperation, and (real) intellectual engagement *with* others.

The book is divided up into five interrelated chapters, including this introduction and a short conclusion. Chapters 2, 3 and 4, which stand at the core, revolve around verbs that are essential in un- and re-thinking the way(s) we communicate around interculturality: *(un-)voicing, scrutinizing, nurturing and galvanizing*. Chapter 2 explores the two central elements of voices and silence in research and education and helps us become aware of the importance of listening to what others have to say (to self, too!) and to the complexities of 'voicing' and 'listening to' (rather than merely *hearing*). It asks questions

12 *Interculturality is dead; long live interculturality!*

such as *what is a voice? How can we represent and reproduce voices? Why do revising and reconsidering voices that we have listened to matter, especially with people involved in our research and education activities?* I have prepared here both theoretical and methodological accounts and activities to support us in thinking further about the centrality of voices, which, I feel, should be the main emphasis of research and education, and thus communicative work for interculturality. The multifaceted notion of silence is discussed as a way of remembering to put things *on hold*.

Chapter 3 is devoted to scrutinizing the ways we engage with interculturality, laying the emphasis first on the (inevitable) ideologization of the notion, and then on language and issues of translation in communicating around interculturality. With these, I wish to 'dig' deeper into very few scholars' calls for placing language at the centre of teaching and research activities in connection to interculturality. The chapter thus helps us reflect further on the important processes of dialoguing, dis-/agreeing, challenging and even 'disturbing the peace'.

Chapter 4 builds upon the two previous chapters in order to make recommendations and proposals as to how communicating around intercultural scholarship and education could nurture (be nurtured) galvanize (be galvanized). I use concrete examples from my own recent research and teaching-supervisory work to do so. Chapter 4 gives some directions for future engagements around interculturality in research and education, but it is not meant to be taken *at face value*. As such, I call for my readers to keep a critical eye on my own ideological takes on communicating around interculturality throughout the book. Criticality of criticality and reflexivity of reflexivity are now inevitable in dealing with interculturality in our polarized world where 'truth' tends to be constructed one-sidedly.

[Reflexive and critical potpourri]

- Reflect on the work of the conductor mentioned at the beginning of the introduction. Do you find it to be a good metaphor for what we do as 'communicators around interculturality'? Can you think of other relevant metaphors?
- What do you make of Shaw's quote for communicating around interculturality: "The single biggest problem in communication is the illusion that it has taken place"?
- What calls for 'interculturality' have you come across recently in different contexts (slogans, keywords, policies)?
- Jot down the types of communicative activities you engage with around interculturality for a day. Which ones do you consider to be un-/successful or improvable and why?
- Do you understand the importance of reflecting on meta-communicating around interculturality instead of merely focusing on how we 'do'

interculturality face-to-face with others? What aspects of this meta-communication would you want to explore in the next chapters?
- How much do you feel concerned about this critique: "Too many publications on the notion 'pretend' to be outside of the sphere of the intercultural encounters and experiences that they describe, problematize and analyse, as if they were exterior to them"? Is this an issue that you often face? What solutions have you found to deal with it?
- Access any inter-/national journal related to interculturality (or its companions) and observe the types of communicative acts that the authors wish to 'do' in the titles of their articles. In the chapter, I noted the use of bridging, capturing, exploring . . . What do the verbs you find tell you about the authors' intentions?
- The topics of voices, silence, scrutinizing, nurturing and galvanizing are discussed in the next chapters to open up discussions about communicating around interculturality. Review each of these keywords one by one and speculate as to what the chapters might contain.

Notes

1 My translation of "La pédagogie de Panula est très concrète. Elle parle des fondamentaux. Quel est le rôle du chef? c'est avant tout aider les musiciens à jouer et à interpréter la musique. Il faut donc une technique précise. Dès le début, il m'a dit d'abandonner tout maniérisme, tout geste superflu. Chaque geste doit être utile au musicien. Le principe de base est le suivant: si on ne peut pas les aider, il faut au moins essayer de ne pas trop les déranger. Ça fait sourire, mais Panula a entièrement raison. Tout peut se résumer à la clarté de la technique des mains et des gestes. La communication des intentions doit être limpide".
2 The constant use of square brackets ([. . .]) in the book aims to place us in different 'compartments' of thinking and reflecting as we unthink and rethink communicating around interculturality. Like a train without a concrete destination and endpoint, we enter an undefined number of compartments, listening in on what multifaceted voices have to say (and silence) about interculturality. The short moments of silence that these brackets represent for the readers urge them to pause to be with themselves and to reflect further on what I am saying in the book.
3 A potpourri is a mixture of dried flowers and leaves used to give a pleasant smell to, e.g., a drawer, a car or a room. It also refers to a miscellaneous collection of ideas.

References

Berkenkotter, C., Bhatia, V. K., & Gotti, M. (Eds.). (2012). *Insights into academic genres*. Peter Lang.
Bibby, T. (2017). *The creative self: Psychoanalysis, teaching and learning in the classroom*. Routledge.
Boulez, P. (1986). *Orientations – collected writings*. Faber & Faber.
Dervin, F. (2016). *Interculturality in education*. Palgrave Macmillan.
Dervin, F. (2022). *Interculturality in fragments*. Springer.
Dervin, F. (2023). *The paradoxes of interculturality*. Routledge.

Dervin, F., & Yuan, M. (2021). *Revitalizing interculturality in education*. Routledge.

Franck, M. (2022). *La technique des mains doit être limpide, pas de geste superflu*. Interview. www.radiofrance.fr/francemusique/podcasts/les-grands-entretiens/mikko-franck-chef-d-orchestre-2-5-4895393

Holmes, P., Reynolds, J., & Ganassin, S. (2022). *The politics of researching multilingually*. Multilingual Matters.

Piller, I. (2010). *Intercultural communication: A critical introduction*. Edinburgh University Press.

Snyder, S., & Fenner, D. S. (2021). *Culturally responsive teaching for multilingual learners*. Corwin.

Victoria, M. (2022). *Methodological issues and challenges in researching transculturally*. Cambridge Scholars Publishing.

Wang, Y. (2022). Tracing the historical development of ethnic colleges and universities to strengthen the consciousness of the Chinese national community. *Journal of Contemporary Educational Research*, 6(5), 135–144.

2 (Un-)voicing

[Vocalizing]

1. When you hear the word *voices* in connection to the notion of interculturality (especially in terms of how we speak about it in research and education), what comes to mind?
2. Do you consider your own voice(s) to be important in the way interculturality is discussed and debated in academia and education? How seriously is it taken by others (e.g., teachers, professors, decision-makers)? Has anyone ever asked you to position yourself towards this complex notion and taken into account your viewpoints?
3. In the chapter, I argue that *silence* is a complex phenomenon that is both needed and problematic. How do you see it in relation to discourses of interculturality in research and education? How often have you considered it?

Throwing voices

> "The voice is a very mysterious instrument. It's in our bodies, and we have very little control over it because the muscles are mostly involuntary".
>
> (Fleming, 2023)

On the Venice home and studio of the Italian composer Luigi Nono (1924–1990) one can read the following inscription: "The master of sound and silence" (*Maestro di suoni e silenzi* in Italian). In order to communicate around interculturality in education and research, I am arguing in this chapter that we need to strive to be the master of *voice* (and *silence*), and especially to learn to 'throw voices'. In English, the idiom to throw (one's) voice refers to the process of *throwing our voice* to sound as if it were coming from a distant location or from some other person or thing. As we shall see here, the complex phenomenon of silence could and should be 'thrown' too.

In my long-term exploration of 'classical music' as inspiration for my work on interculturality, I came across a piece that I have kept coming back

DOI: 10.4324/9781003451938-2

to over the years: *The Human Voice*, an opera written by Francis Poulenc (1899–1963), based on a text by Jean Cocteau (1930). The famous Spanish film director Pedro Almodóvar released a half-hour free adaptation of *The Human Voice* with Tilda Swinton in 2020. The 40-minute opera, a one-hander, deals with heartbreak and emotional shifts in interactions with other people, showcasing moments of rage and vulnerability through the pulse and pace of the singer's *voices*. In the libretto, a woman (*elle – she* in the French language) is on the phone with her former lover, who just broke up with her. The line keeps playing up and breaking, and other phone users are connected to her by mistake. Elle's wounded soul is palpable in the constant repetition of 'Hellos!', her mixing of platitudes, accusations and threats. One of the most famous lines from the opera is uttered by Elle towards the end of the piece: "If you cut the conversation, you cut the air".

As I was doing some research around the complex and fascinating topics of voice and silence for this book, I realized that, in some countries, some professors specialize in 'voice' and are referred to as 'Voice Professors'. Catherine Cook, an American mezzo-soprano, is on the 'Voice Faculty' at the San Francisco Conservatory of Music in the U.S. and holds a Distinguished Chair in Voice (Cook, 2023). As part of her teaching, she supports students for proper vocal technique, guiding them about the functioning of the voice, healthy sounds leading to registration, resonance, support and avoiding damages to the voice. Students' individual needs in terms of voice range, volume and navigating chest voice to head voice, are met through specific exercises. Reading about what a Voice Professor like Cook does, I became convinced that anyone involved with interculturality (researchers, teachers, students) should learn and teach voices around the notion to be able to enrich theirs and others' takes. As such, communicating around interculturality also requires *throwing voices*: articulating, playing with and manipulating voices (amongst others). This chapter problematizes this important aspect while discussing the importance of silence as a central component of (un-)voicing.

[*What is a voice?* Most dictionaries would list at least three understandings of the word in English:

> The sounds that are made when people speak or sing.
> (The right to) an expression of opinion.
> An important quality or opinion that someone expresses, or the person who is able to express it.
>
> (Cambridge Dictionary, 2023)

The voice thus has to do with physical sounds emitted by humans but also with the idea of opinion. Etymologically the word comes from Latin and Proto-Indo-European for words related to speaking, crying and language. Voice has come to adopt the aforementioned different meanings over the centuries. For instance, Etymonline (2023) reminds us that voice as an 'ability in a singer' dates back to 1600, while voice in the context of insanity (hearing voices) dates from 1911.

In Finnish the word *ääni* means *voice and sound,* but also *vote* (in elections, the meaning is derived from Swedish). Whenever I pronounce the word *ääni*, with the 'floating' repetition of *ä* at the beginning, I always feel somehow the complex sound of a voice.]

[It is telling that in the English language – and in some other languages – many idioms relate to voice, indicating the centrality of the word for our intricate identity-making *with and for others*, hinting at the instabilities and transformations that we all experience on a daily basis. Some examples in English:

- *To be in good/poor voice*: to sound appealing/unpleasant (to others!);
- *Voice within you* refers to one's conscience telling us that we are doing something wrong;
- *Talk to hear (the sound of) (one's) voice*: to sound arrogant and boasting; to talk without purpose;
- *Voice crying in the wilderness*: expressing an unpopular idea or opinion.]

As social beings, we 'throw' our voices all the time, borrowing from others, pretending to sound like others, while being judged at the same time for what and how we project ideas, opinions and words.

[Voices get constantly judged for what they utter and for their appearances and qualities. As such, voices can be said to be *boomy, breathy, gruff, nasal, purring, soft-spoken, strangulated, toned . . .* Different traits and connotations can be attributed (often wrongly) to the ways voices sound.]

Before we problematize the idea of *voice* further, let us briefly consider examples of how the word has been used in research on intercultural communication education:

> As a general use, the word *voice* seems to have been utilized to refer to large entities such as civilizations (Dallmayr's, 2003 *Dialogue Among Civilizations: Some Exemplary Voices* where Ibn Rushd and Gadamer are discussed), specific groups of individuals such as children (Ingoglia et al., 2021), in relation to democratic and intercultural competences in the primary school context (Caetano et al., 2020), about children and young people in the development of intercultural education – participatory projects and international students in higher education (Jones, 2009). In *Our Voices: Essays in Culture, Ethnicity, and Communication* (Gonzalez & Chen, 2015), 'diverse' individuals recount their personal experiences of interculturality by presenting student-oriented readings. The book blurb (Gonzalez & Chen, 2015) explains: "Praised by students for its abundance of short, first-person narratives, Our Voices traverses topics as diverse as queer identity, racial discourse, and codes of communication in nontraditional families".

18 *(Un-)voicing*

In our times of 'decolonizing' knowledge, many scholars and educators are now calling for voices beyond the 'West' (the 'West' is still dominating the field, as we will keep noticing in the book) to be included more systematically and coherently in research and education. Maldona and Lazrus (2019) refer to "the voices and wisdom of Indigenous peoples", as well as to their observations, insights and knowledge, as 'Rising Voices'. The same applies to Burgess et al. (2023), from the Australian context, in a chapter where they urge listening to 'Aboriginal Voices' in creating a world worth living in and placing Aboriginal-informed knowledge, leadership and practices at the centre. Mudaly and Sanjigadu (2022) call for voices from the Global South to be 'reclaimed' as far as epistemic production and dissemination are concerned. Finally, *Critical Autoethnography and Intercultural Learning: Emerging Voices* (Stanley, 2020) includes storytelling and analyses from emerging scholars of 'diverse' backgrounds and communities focusing on the influence of personal experience on teaching and learning in relation to interculturality.

This brief look at how the very word *voices* seems to be used in scholarship published in English related to intercultural communication education indicates that the word seems to refer to 'mere' (under-/privileged) research participants whose voices are mediated by a researcher, and to calls for unheard/silenced voices to be included in current scholarship – as is the case in most strands of the human and social sciences today.

In what follows, we deepen our exploration of voice in order for us to reflect on *communicating around*. Research and education are all about voices being used on stage (e.g., in the classroom or a book) and backstage (e.g., in one's office preparing a lecture or writing) by thousands of different individuals. Being a scholar and an educator means accepting maneuvering different voices, ours and others'.

Voices are everywhere around us; they interpenetrate each other in more or less obvious ways; voices connect us to other worlds (past/present/future; politics; the economy) beyond our own self. Voices can be spoken, written, symbolized, drawn, repeated by a machine . . . [How much of what we say and write is actually ours?]

In China, I have often seen similar calligraphy documents as the one in Figure 2.1, which symbolizes well, I believe, the complexity and enmeshing of voices in and around us. This is an old Chinese book, containing a printed text in black, entered into columns, which are meant to be read from right to left, top-down. Applied to the page, one can see red 'seals' of differing sizes, with a large square one on the top right side. I have often seen such red seals on different kinds of calligraphies and works of art in China. In my own 'corner' of the world, one rarely writes or adds anything to such old documents. What the red seals indicate on the Chinese document is former ownerships –

(Un-)voicing 19

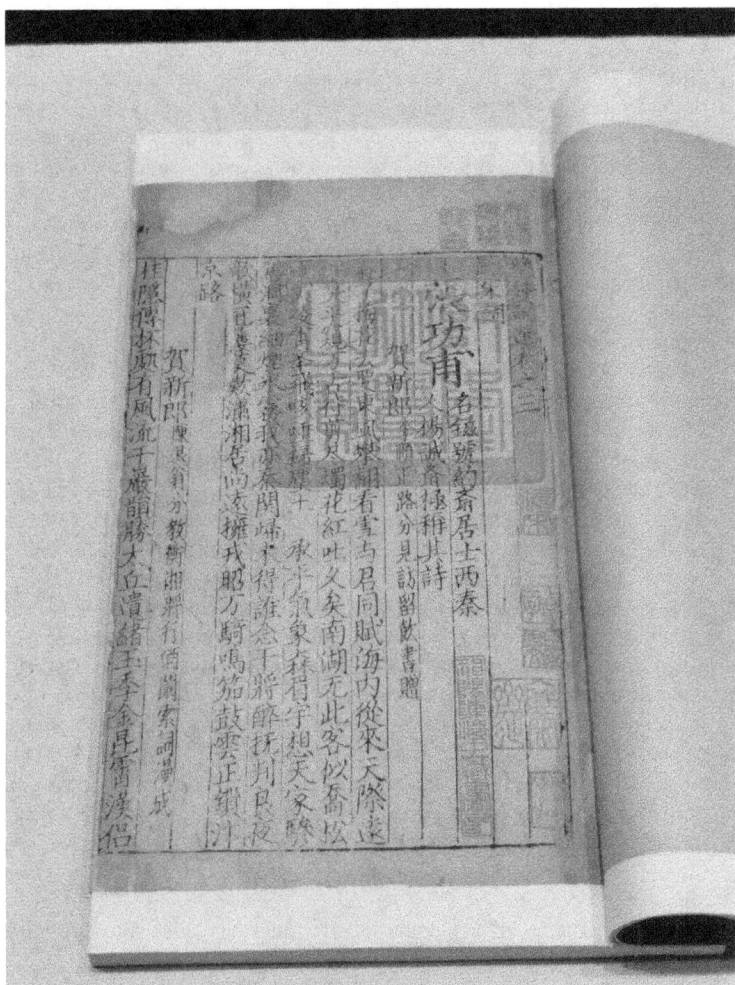

Figure 2.1 The multivoicedness of an ancient Chinese book

the one who bought the piece applies their seal to it. So, when one sees an old calligraphy or work of art in China, one not only hears the 'voice' of the one who created it but also the different hands, mouths and ears that consulted it over the years. As such, the 'archeology' of the piece become multivoiced. This represents a very fitting symbol to discuss the complexities of voices.

a. My own work on interculturality has been inspired by Bakhtin (1981) and enunciative pragmatics (Angermuller, 2014) for about two decades (Dervin, 2008). First, these have helped me explore how others deal with, do and speak of interculturality. For the past three years, I have pushed for exploring what is often labelled as 'dialogism' in the very work of the scholar and educator, enriching our takes on such a complex and flexible notion as interculturality. A few words about dialogism will suffice here. Bakhtin's work on literature conceptualizes discourse as consisting of multiple in-/direct voices, claiming that all that we utter is always in dialogue with what was said before by people around us or other broader entities such as governments, ways of recalling history, marketing voices . . . Even if one might be speaking in a monologue, one always makes use of others' voices, and thus one is always dialogic.
b. In my voice(s), there is always your voice(s), their voice(s), our voice(s). My voice is your voice; your voice is my voice. All these voices are, in fact, inseparable, and we may not be aware of this omnipresence. At times, we create boundaries between these voices in what we say, represent and do. We might, for instance, make a direct reference to a friend's voice in what we say. We might also place boundaries between our voices, blocking some, erasing their origins.
c. In his story called *'reusement* (Leiris, 1997), a French word he coined for shortening 'fortunately' as (for) *'tunately*, Michel Leiris explains that, when he was a child, he was made aware of the power of others' voices when he dropped a lead soldier and, as he retrieved it and was relieved that it was not broken, he uttered "'reusement (fortunately!)". His entourage corrected him straight away, saying that he should say *heureusement*. This came as a shock to little Leiris, who had been using the shortened version until then. Troubled by the imposition of the 'correct' version, he reflects on the power of language and especially on the disrupting power of the other. [*We are spoken to by other voices as much as we speak these other voices. Our voices get embedded in others' voices constantly.*]
d. I/we/they quote, I/we/they translate, I/we/they dis-agree, but I/we/they also misunderstand and misuse others' voices.

In research on interculturality – like in other fields . . .

> . . . I/we/they quote/recycle the most cited (and thus dominating) voices– the most popular voices (which tend to be from the 'West' today, from English speakers). I/we/they cite arguments, concepts, research results, and ideologies ('small cultures'; 'democratic culture'; 'intercultural competence' . . .). These voices are guru-like, savior-like, the untouchables. They give me/you/us the impression/illusion of being empowered to publish or speak. If these voices have spoken in a specific way, then doing the

same, mimicking them cannot but give me/you/us power. I/we/they never engage critically with their voices since they are considered as the 'voice master'. I/we/they communicate around these voices but rarely in deep, critical terms. They are just accepted, followed and serve as the 'truth' (e.g., *Bourdieu, Byram, Dervin, Holliday, Kramsch, Piller, Said*). [Am I essentializing these voices and those who use them (or not)?]

... The power of these voices means that many voices are unpopular and dominated, disregarded, silenced or unheard in global research. We are also told that there are voices to be avoided. We thus reject some of these voices consciously (e.g., Hofstede, Huntington). Some of these voices have become politically incorrect, pariahs of interculturality – even if we haven't really read them, we avoid making any reference to them. Or if we do, we only include them to 'discard' them.

... I/we/they misquote others, either misunderstanding or simplifying what they have to say about interculturality. I/we/they include them because I/we/they feel that they have to be included. I/we/they also feel obliged to do so, being a member of, e.g., a specific tribe. Their voices thus become incomplete, manipulated, but made to fit our agendas. I/we/they give them our voice, too, by citing them, which increases their power to dominate.

... I/we/they corrupt, steal and camouflage certain voices to avoid having to admit that they have inspired me/us/them. As such, instead of citing a scholar I/we/they don't like, I/we/they use another scholar (e.g., *B* instead of *Dervin* for a reference on *identity in interculturality*, since the latter does not belong to our own tribe).

... I/we/they cite voices in English mostly.Unvoicing interculturality is an object of research and education spoken about in hundreds of languages on a daily basis. I/we/they don't even try to include what I (could) read in other languages.

e. Ideologies are omnipresent in everything that we do (see Chapter 3). We often talk and act in specific ways, following ideological orders and agendas – without always realizing it. Ideologies are found in thousands of voices that are undecipherable. They are there in us. They have been passed onto us by institutions, texts and other people. They have become part of us, and they govern the way we speak, what we say and do. At times, they make us forget our own voice(s). We speak, but we don't know what we mean; we are not even sure if we disagree with what we say, including these ideologies. I am thinking here of the use of concepts such as *culture* or *community*, which are often found in this automatic way of engaging with interculturality, which I have called *interculturalspeak* (Dervin, 2016). I have asked colleagues and students on many occasions to explain *why* they include these words in what they have to say about interculturality – I never ask them to define them since their multilingual polysemy and specific ideological inclusion will never satisfy us in defining them. In all cases, as much as I would be incapable of explaining why I might be tempted to use them in certain (lazy) situations, my interlocutors never can. Whenever we misuse these terms, we demonstrate a simple principle around voices: what we say tells more about what we do not say. We are not in control of our own voice and of the ones we (mis-)use. At the same time, not being able to explain why we use these voices for specific purposes (e.g., *culture* to replace other terms we are not supposed to use or of which we are not in control, such as *race* or *money*) reminds us that communicating around interculturality should recognize that we cannot always achieve this goal and, as we shall see later, accept retraction into silence.

f. I/we/they are urged to speak and communicate all the time in academia and education. There is rarely a moment of quietude and silence. [So many voices are used, played around and manipulated on a daily basis!]. I/we/they are asked to publish, disseminate, speak and guide even if I/we/they have nothing (new) to say. I/we/they jump at some selected voices to find something to say (e.g., *decolonizing, translanguaging, essentialism* . . .). I/we/they do not necessarily aim to say something new since I/we/they do not always know much about these topics or are unaware of their archaeology. So I/we/they tend to repeat the same voices, thus the same concepts, arguments, results and ideologies in English, thus ignoring other (multilingual, disruptive) voices. Interculturality is unstable, flexible and complex. The voices that represent it in research and education should follow these patterns and processes instead of recycling the same voices.

[Are my own words about interculturality *ever* mine?]

g. How about our own voices? Since what we think, say, negotiate and co-construct about interculturality is embedded in constant change, can our own voices be coherent and consistent? I have often found myself in the same situation as composer Kurtag (2009, p. 35) when he was asked about something he had said about one of his creations called *Játékok*:

Interviewer:	Then I also found another quote. I don't know if it's from you or why it's in German. It seems that you said about *Játékok*: "A kind of mythology of everyday life, an attempt to tame the diabolical forces of everyday life". Is it possible that you said that?
GK:	It's not . . . Not impossible, no idea.
Interviewer:	But this thought is not foreign to you.
GK:	No.[1]

A few months ago, someone reminded me of something that I had written back in 2015 and asked me to develop this idea. I confessed that I had forgotten ever having 'voiced' this idea and that, in any case, I disagreed entirely with the argument that I had put forward in the past and deconstructed it – to the dismay of my interlocutor.

Lies, small and big lies. For Camus (1970, p. 336), "Lying is not only saying what isn't true. It is also, in fact especially, saying more than is true and, in the case of the human heart, saying more than one feels. We all do it, every day, to make life simpler". Ethics is central in research and education, and thus lies are rarely discussed in these contexts. When I/we/they read a paper or listen to a lecture, I/we/they assume that the utterer is telling *the* – or some – truth. And in most cases, they certainly are trying to speak as close as they can to what they consider to be the truth. However, since I/we/they are asked to maneuver others' voices, embedded in specific geo-economic-political ideological contexts, I/we/they can never be sure that what is discussed is *a truth*. An ideological call to speak about interculturality in a specific way always pushes us on the verge of lying. [If I am located in the Philippines, and I want to make use of Byram's democratic culture or intercultural citizenship; if I am located in Uganda, and I want to make use of Baker's transcultural ideology; if I am located in Finnish Lapland, and I want to make use of essentialism; am I going to be 'lying' by making believe that all these ideologies can be copied and pasted onto the very specific glocal context that I work from? Will I be saying too much about what is occurring in my own context? Will I be silencing some voices by putting these words onto my own people?]

Academic voices are stylistic, too, although they often have to follow strict guidelines in terms of what and how things can be said and for what reasons. One often speaks of academic rigor, avoiding biases, etc. These all refer to how to deal with and organize the interplay between voices somehow. Academic voices are always peer-reviewed, which means that many voices are always imbricated in one given voice. Developing one's own style and voice should be a central component of what we do when communicating around interculturality. Often, we copy the way(s) others express themselves – we speak in their 'voices'. Often, it is difficult to see that boundary, and I am very much convinced that the way I write, speak and communicate around interculturality contains many elements from the thousands of scholars, thinkers, artists and writers whom I have consulted. However, I am well aware that, over the years, I have developed a stylistic voice that has its own characteristics (maybe). Moving away from mostly Western conventions of presenting one's thoughts and ideas, which seems to me to be still very 'rational' and 'objectifying'. My use of fragment format writing, allowing me to jump from one idea to another, which may not go hand in hand, or from one style of writing to another, was inspired by the idea that interculturality never follows a straight line. This way of constructing my voice, communicating with thousands of other voices, tests our resistance to the instabilities and incoherencies experienced when communicating with others – and thus accepting our complex places in the world.

To finish this section on voices, I add a list of six concepts that can support us in thinking further about the centrality of voices in relation to communicating around interculturality. These appear in alphabetical order in what follows, with no hierarchy of importance.

[*Doxa* and *vox populi*]

These two Latin words have to do with the voice of the crowd. Doxa translates as common belief and popular opinion and is found in words like heterodoxy (beliefs, ideas or activities different to and even opposed to the generally accepted) and orthodoxy (belief/adherence to creeds). In Greek doxa has to do with opinion, praise, glory and honour. Vox populi, from Latin, refers to the voice of the people, i.e., an idea or a belief accepted by most people. These two phrases urge us to reflect on what we think and believe in, and especially on the origins of our beliefs, ideas and activities. When it comes to interculturality, many elements that we push forward and use come from the doxa and/or the vox populi, passed on to us by other scholars, educators, books, etc.

Today, I consider the use of certain concepts and ideas, such as *culture, culture shock and stereotype*, to be part of the doxa and vox populi of interculturality. We need to unpack these terms and reflect on their origins and why we (still) use them in research and education. At the same time, we need to listen carefully to how they are used outside academia and education to interrogate their meanings and purposes.

[Gamelan]

Gamelan is a form of music which finds its origins in the Indonesian islands of Java and Bali. Different kinds of instruments are used for playing it: *drums, gongs, metal instruments struck with mallets, flutes* and *stringed instruments*. It can also be sung. Gamelan can accompany theatrical performances and include mantras, offerings, or dance.

It is often misnamed as an orchestra in the 'Western' sense of the word, but it is not an orchestra as such. Although it is played with many instruments together, Gamelan can be referred to as a 'collective instrument' which is highly polyphonic (multipart) and heterophonic (one part varies a melody played simultaneously in another part), spinning and weaving sounds between themselves in what resembles a sound bath rather than 'mere' music to listen to. When they play, the Gamelan instrumentalists share melodic and rhythmic motives instead of focusing on notes on one specific instrument. As such, multiple instruments can play interlocking parts to form a single rhythm. This creates a collective instrument with complex textures and layers of voices, which cannot always be identified separately. To make it more concrete, one could imagine that Gamelan players cut a piano into different parts, each playing only the notes available on their own keys. I note that Gamelan has no partition and no conductor. The players just engage with each other by ear.

The Gamelan is a great metaphor to rethink the ways we make use of different voices when communicating around interculturality, beyond the work of the conductor and of a pre-programmed partition.

[Hocketing]

In medieval polyphonic (choir) music, hocketing alternated between parts, single and/or groups of notes, leading to a continuous flow with one voice sounding and another one being silenced for a while. As soon as a voice stops, another one starts, and vice versa. Polyphony emerges from this interplay of voices. French composer Guillaume de Machaut (c. 1300–1377) made use of this technique extensively. Austrian composer Anton Webern (1883–1945) used a similar technique for instruments in his compositions, creating swift, single-noted instrumental textures.

Hocket is another suited metaphor for rethinking the way we communicate around interculturality and especially for reflecting on voice shifts.

[Polymusic]

Polymusic happens when musicians do not synchronize or interact while playing a piece of music – a technique often used in music composition today, which allows spaces of conflict and friction. Examples of polymusic include music pieces such as *The Gong on the Hook and Ladder or Firemen's Parade on Main Street* by Charles Ives (1904–1934) and American band The Shaggs' *Things I wonder* (2016).

Voices need to clash and confront each other to create new effects and interesting ideas. This is again very inspiring for interculturalspeak – although the idea of clashes is avoided in research and education today, I do insist on reflecting on what this could add to the way we work on interculturality.

[Prosopopoeia]

A figure of speech in which an absent or imaginary person or thing is represented as speaking. Prosopopoeia allows its users to adopt the voice of others. From Greek for *face/person* and to *make/to do*, i.e., *giving face*. One can use direct discourse or indirect discourse to represent others or things.

[Puppetry]

Human manipulation of a figure representing an animal or a person in some kind of theatrical show. Manipulating a figure often requires ventriloquizing, which is defined as:

> Ventriloquism, or ventriloquy, is an act of stagecraft in which a person (a ventriloquist) changes his or her voice so that it appears that the voice

is coming from elsewhere, usually a puppeteered 'dummy'. Ventriloquism thus problematizes the question as to who or even what is speaking or, more generally, saying or doing something in a given situation. (Simpson & Dervin, 2017)

Inserting voices in our ways of communicating around interculturality might often have to do with ventriloquism – we repeat, recycle, parrot.

Pause

The topic of voices forces us to pause and think about the polygonal 'noise' around us. We 'throw voices', which might reverberate; others also 'throw voices' at us, others, the world, their locality, through the media, journal articles, keynote speeches, lectures . . . Some of these voices appear to be more meaningful to us and to others, while others are ignored, censored, or discarded. For example, when I read research articles, some voices I hear and read, but I feel I don't really hear them or I hear them too often (again). My desire to communicate with a text or another scholar often gets 'frustrated' at the lack of *voicing beyond* the (unfair) over-voiced . . .

[I hear you, but I don't understand you. Each word seems to make sense individually, but collectively they confuse me.]

[I hear you, and I think I understand you. However, I am not sure if what you say means what I mean.]

[I hear you, and I know that your words look familiar to me but mean something different.]

Voices for interculturality should go beyond 'mere' academia, and we should be eager to listen to artists, philosophers, people on the streets. In my life, all these voices have often pulled me in different directions.

I argue that a lack of serious reflection on (un-)voicing can lead to *incommunicado* around interculturality. *Incommunicado* comes from Spanish and Latin and refers to a situation not allowing communication or without means of communication.

4'33

The title of this subsection is a reference to a musical composition for piano by American composer John Cage (1952). During the premiere, the pianist sat quietly at his piano for four minutes and thirty-three seconds in complete silence without touching the piano keys. Cage (2022, p. 3) wrote about the performance: "You could hear the wind stirring outside during the first movement. During the second, raindrops began pattering the roof, and during the third people themselves made all kinds of interesting sounds as they talked or walked out". With 4'33, Cage wanted people to reflect on the hierarchy of sounds that they had been fed, considering all kinds of sounds around them as music instead of the potential piano music. This instant of music was not necessarily appreciated by all audience members, and yet it became a classic over time.

In this section, I wish to tackle the issue of silence in communication. In the constant flow and flood of words that we as educators and researchers need to consume, produce and watch increase, it is important to take a break to unthink and rethink what it is that we (are asked to) do and say about interculturality. (4'33^2) [I want to make a reference here to Samuel Beckett's work and to how his writing has inspired the American composer Morton Feldman. In his play entitled *Happy Days* (2010), a woman, Winnie, chatters to herself about the trivialities of daily life while literally sinking into the ground until she is buried up to her neck. She is desperate to communicate, e.g., through reciting poetry (but she is scared of "forgetting her classics" and remembering a better past) in an endless monologue. Her husband, Willie (note the puns on the characters' names, with references to win and will), is sitting behind her, answering her questions in monosyllabic and disconnected ways. He appears not to be listening to her, and yet, faced with (his) silence, his wife continues talking. Winnie has no real interlocutor with whom to reciprocate. At some point in the play, she remarks that "someone is looking at me still", as if she was satisfied that silence was overcome by the mere presence of someone else. As the play moves on, Winnie's body disappears in the sand, leaving her with words only as signs of existence. But her speech becomes more hesitant and disjointed, her "words fail", and she becomes even more vulnerable, hinting at the limitations of language to express feelings and face anxiety. The play ends with the famous words: "What's it mean? What's it meant to mean"? – emphasizing failing expression. Morton Feldman was very much inspired by Beckett's work, and in his 'anti-opera' called *Neither* (1976), the limitations of language to communicate become obvious too. The piece starts with music only since Feldman was waiting for the words that Beckett was writing for the opera when he started writing the piece – which he had agreed to reluctantly since he admitted he did not like opera and was not eager to see his words used for such an art form. Feldman told Beckett that he had rarely used words in his compositions and that he had written "vocal pieces without words" (Tubridy, 2010). The libretto by Beckett ended up containing a few sentences such as "To and fro in shadow from inner to outershadow from impenetrable self to impenetrable unself by way of neither" (Tubridy, 2010, p. 145). The voice of the singer appears slowly in the anti-opera, sounding like *parlando* (a speaking voice) without a melody. Spaces of silence increase as we move into the 47-minute piece. When *Neither* was premiered, only the face of the singer was seen (which was reminiscent of Winnie). In a similar vein as *Happy Days*, the singing becomes more and more fragmented and stumbling as we move towards the end of the piece, silence taking over. Both *Happy Days* and *Neither* always remind me of my work as both a scholar and an educator of interculturality: I stumble over my words; I don't understand myself and others; I don't feel that I/we/they are communicating; I/we/they are urged to speak, but I/we/they want to be quiet.] (4'33) [A short poem by Jeffrey McDaniel also urges us to reconsider silence in communication. In 'The Quiet World', McDaniel (1998) tells us that the government is limiting the number of words that people can use on a daily basis (77 words). The narrator explains how he uses these words and saves some for his lover. He explains:

> When she doesn't respond,
>   I know she's used up all her words,
>   so I slowly whisper *I love you*
>   thirty-two and a third times.
>   After that, we just sit on the line
>   and listen to each other breathe.

With the 'culture' of short messages, short articles and short books of today, each word is valuable but also potentially meaningless. I am not personally on 'Western' social media because I don't like to be urged to speak even if I have nothing to say. My absence from Twitter, TikTok and the like, enriches my mind with silence.] (4'33) [How has research on interculturality dealt with silence? – one might ask. Somehow, I feel that the topic is not extensively discussed today. Here are some snapshots of what I/you/we have been writing about. One main strand of research on silence and interculturality has to do with teaching-learning: In 2023 Su, Wood and Tribe proposed silence as a positive pedagogical approach in schools, arguing that in the 'West' silence is avoided in favour of talk – with the triad of talking, thinking and learning being put forward systematically. Based on a systematic review of journals, the authors examine how much importance is given to silence as a pedagogical approach in different parts of the world, noticing differences. The authors related silence to power and critical pedagogy in the paper. In *Silence in Intercultural Communication: Perceptions and Performance*, Nakane (2017) discusses how and why silence is used, misused and perceived interculturally, focusing on different levels of communication and social levels of social organization. The author also revises the stereotype of the 'silent Asian' – considering silence often leads to stereotypes. In a similar vein, Wang et al. (2022) focus on the social practice of silence at a U.K. university, urging readers to reconsider international students' participation and the merits of silence in pedagogy. In a chapter of the book entitled *Academic Experiences of International Students in Chinese Higher Education*, Brown and O'Brien (2020) have a chapter entitled 'The significance of silence'. In the chapter about a Sino-foreign university venture, they explore perceptions of silence between international students, local students and their professors. Their findings question essentialist interpretations of, e.g., the 'silent Chinese', opening up new discussions around silence as a 'problem' in international education.

Following the trend of decolonizing knowledge and interculturality, Cohen (2022) discusses the ways 'cultural dialogue' was colonized, making a reference to 'the silence of Miskito Prince' (a story from the narrative of a freed slave). In the book, the author reflects on ways of having an intercultural conversation in the humanities when these are products of coloniality. Focusing on five concepts used to imagine how to deal with this issue (understanding, cosmopolitanism, piety, reciprocity and patience), Cohen suggests new vocabulary for analyzing past intercultural interactions, arguing for new ways of engaging in scholarly conversations around interculturality beyond silencing.

Outside the very literature on interculturality, many exciting editorial projects have dealt with silence. *Silence as Language: Verbal Silence as a Means of Expression* by Ephratt (2022) is one of them. In the book, the author discusses multiple aspects of the role of silence in language, arguing that silence is as communicative in language as speech. He also asserts that silence serves multiple purposes, such as activating the addresser, conveying emotions and informing. Freeden's (2022) book *Concealed Silences and Inaudible Voices in Political Thinking* explores how silences occur in politics and serves as a highly flexible power resource. Bao's (2023) *Silence in English Language Pedagogy: From Research to Practice* problematizes what he considers a highly debatable concept, discusses online silence in education and presents trends in silence research. Finally, in the field of music, Voit (2022) proposes an ontology of silence, problematizing their multifaceted relationships. For instance, he explains that silence is used today as pauses but also compositional material.] (4'33) The paradox of using so many words to discuss silence in communicating around silence is often defined as absence of sound or noise. [We are also told in many languages that silence is gold. The country where I live, Finland, has been marketing itself as a 'heaven of silence' since the 2010s. Everything starts and finishes with silence. Silence itself is often considered as language, and in a noisy world like ours, silence can never be *real* silence. Looking for complete silence is an impossibility somehow since there is always a trace of a sound in silence. *As such, how do we ask for silence without making some noise?* Many thinkers have reflected on this complex phenomenon. For the philosopher Camus (1991, p. 256) "The world is never quiet, even its silence eternally resounds with the same notes, in vibrations which escape our ears. As for those that we perceive, they carry sounds to us, occasionally a chord, never a melody". John Cage (1961, p. 8) argues similarly, "There is no such thing as an empty space or an empty time. There is always something to see, something to hear. In fact, try as we may to make a silence, we cannot". Silence is never possible. Breathing, coughing, rustling, scratching, sighing and squeaking are always soundlessly there in us and in others. Silence today symbolizes inequality. As such not everybody has access to the same type of 'quality' silence and time for it. Silence can be considered a commodity (see the sale of expensive 'noise-canceling headphones'). During the COVID-19 pandemic in the 'West', while the privileged could 'hide' quietly and silently in their homes, many under-privileged still had to continue rushing around, exposing themselves and their families to the deadly virus. What is more, many people in the world don't have the space or the time to enjoy silence. I also note that many are, in fact, afraid of silence, of the emptiness that it might represent for them and wish to avoid it as much as they can, preferring to bury themselves in noises and voices.] (4'33) [The first individual whom we meet in silence is self. Silence provides us the space for meditation, self-dialogues/imagined-represented dialogues with others. For Blanchot (1995, pp. 20–21), "And to be silent is still to speak. Silence is impossible". In our silence, we still communicate. We still make some noise and manipulate voices in our heads.] (4'33) [Although having access to silence could be perceived as moments of privilege for some of us, and while others dislike and run away from it, silencing can also refer to violent acts of shutting others up. As such, ideologies, especially dominating ones, which are understood here as orders to do and think, and (hidden) agendas lead to silencing ideologies of which we may not be aware. In communicating around interculturality, as will be seen in the next chapter, current strong 'Western' ideologies of democratic culture, translanguaging and even decolonizing *à la Western* take so much space in research and education that other ideologies are inaudible. Finally, I argue that a given dominating ideology is silent too in the sense that it does not need to communicate with others.] (4'33) [Ghosting, or abruptly ending communication with someone online, e.g,. blocking them from our social media, is a highly violent form of silence. In similar ways, the neoliberal ideology of academic 'publish or perish' can lead to ferocious silence.] (4'33) [For the Chinese author Lu Xun (in Yang, 2016, p. 53): 不在沉默中爆发，就在沉默中灭亡 – which can translate as "If you don't explode in silence, you perish in silence" or "Do not erupt in silence, perish in silence". In other words: *speak up!*] (4'33) [I am always surprised to notice how many people are insensitive to noise in a place like Beijing. During my stays in the capital, sitting on a park bench to read, I get frustrated by people passing me, listening to their radio on their loudspeakers (very loud) and shouting to others. I have often felt that 'our' tolerance for noises, voices and silences differs so much, probably due to the different family and societal structures, the fact that people live in a megacity compared to living in a small city like Turku in Finland. I realized that I spent most of the COVID-19 pandemic time all by myself, just connecting to people on social media, away from crowds and individuals, buried in my silent bubble, which I have found very inspiring for reading, writing and self-reflecting. I do realize that many other people do not feel the same about this kind of silence and prefer to meet others face-to-face and be surrounded by crowds. Would I sound ethnocentric or egocentric quoting Blaise Pascal (2003, p. 45) here: "I have often said that the sole cause of man's unhappiness is that he does not know how to stay quietly in his room"?] (4'33) [Being silent with others is often perceived as clumsy and embarrassing. To be able to listen to others is a skill that has to do with silence. To be able to be silent with someone is a skill I consider to be important to communicate around interculturality. To be able to (re-)negotiate (through) silence with someone matters. Since silence is always the last word, we need to alternate it with audible voices.] (4'33) [Silence in communicating around interculturality in research and education:

- Think for and with ourselves;
- Pause;
- Remove ideologies we disagree with for a while;
- Communicate with self and others quietly and for a longer period;
- Reconsider our beliefs and values;
- Resist the dominant;
- Stop the constant flow of recycled voices.] (4'33)

[To finish on the subject of silence as inspiration for communicating around interculturality, let me introduce two German concepts which can push us to think further: *Fragmante-Stille* and *Generalpause*. *Stille* means silence in German. The idea of *Fragmante-Stille* was put forward by the composer Nono (the 'Master of sound and silence' from the beginning of this chapter) to describe pieces of music composed of music moments ('fragments') articulated by silences of the same duration. As I have put forward fragment-writing for interculturality (Dervin, 2022, 2023), whereby short and concise statements of different kinds about interculturality help us reflect on the notion in a non-linear manner while pushing for the multiplication of (potentially contradictory) ideas, arguments and ideologies, *Fragmante-Stille* requests silence between each fragment to give us space to think, unthink and rethink the content of each fragment, the communication taking place in, around and between them. *Generalpause* is another German term used to describe silences imposed on an entire orchestra in a music score. I believe that we need such *Generalpause* in the way we (mis-)(non-) communicate around interculturality in education and research.

[Many aspects of what this book could be about are silenced because I cannot express fully or precisely what I want to say to you, my reader. My communicating about communicating is doomed to fail.]

[Reflexive and critical potpourri]

- Read a text (any text) about interculturality and try to *imagine, smell, feel, taste, touch* the voices in (and beyond) what you hear. Do the same while you are communicating with someone around interculturality.

- Choose some of the most popular voices that you have used to write, teach and talk about interculturality (scholars, philosophers, educators, writers . . .). If you haven't met them or have no idea what they look like, can you try to imagine what communicating with them face-to-face might be like?
- Listen to people talking about interculturality as an object of research and education. What difference does it seem to make if you are (not) looking at the utterers?
- Here are excerpts from a course description organized online by Shanghai International Studies University (2023, China). Stop on every word that they use to talk about the course objectives and learning outcomes. Whose voice(s) can you (not) hear (famous scholars', teachers', colleagues' . . .)? Are you clear about what they might mean with these elements?

"On this course you'll learn how to become aware your own and others' cultural identities, cultural assumptions we each carry, the nuances of cross-cultural interaction, and their potential for (mis)understanding and growth".

"By the end of the course, you'll be able to . . . (. . .)

Identify cultural variations in communication styles.

Classify some major cultural values underlying different behaviors.

Apply these for adaptation in intercultural interactions more confidently and resourcefully".

"Social perceptions of stereotypes, prejudice, and discrimination related to intergroup contact".

"Variations and perceptions of typical communication behaviors or practices and taxonomies for understanding context, space, time and other contextual factors (Hi-low Context, Proxemics, Monochronic-Polychronic, Silence)".

- An *audiobiography* is an autobiography based on how sounds, voices and silences have shaped who we are, our lives and thinking (amongst others). If you could perform your own audiobiography in relation to the way you see interculturality, what sounds, voices and silences (amongst others) would you include and why? As an example, I would include a clip of French scholar Martine Abdallah-Pretceille talking about the French ideology of secularism; Zygmunt Bauman reflecting on liquid identity; the sound of silence in my summer house in Finland; Chinese students I have worked with over the past years, discussing the ideologies of Chinese Minzu and 'European' democratic culture, in both Chinese and English.

[Recommended reading]

Leiris, M. (1997). *Scratches*. Johns Hopkins University Press.

This is the first volume of the ethnographer's autobiography in which he investigates the language of his childhood. Leiris is considered a forerunner of 20th-century confessional literature. In *Scratches*, many chapters revolve around words and turns of phrase that he misheard or misunderstood and describe his 'initiation into language' (Evans, 2017). Leiris is very much inspiring for reflecting on the way we miscommunicate around interculturality and especially on the influence of others on the way we speak about the notion.

Beckett, S. (2010). *Happy days*. Faber & Faber.

This play by Samuel Beckett was first produced in 1960 in the English language and then translated into French by the author. In *Happy Days*, the main character is buried in a mound of sand, her body disappearing as the play moves on. All she has is *her words*. In a constant flow of monological words, Winnie, the character, reflects on the meanings of language and shares her desire to be heard. Silence here is noisy for the character and the silence that she gets in response to her words reflects the tragedy of breakdowns in communication and the difficulty in accepting the pleasure and treasure of silence – to be with oneself! Winnie keeps lamenting about 'how words fail' – a fact of life that silence can help us celebrate in a world obsessed with (often fake) 'successful' communication. At the end of the play, Winnie asks, "What's it mean? What's it meant to mean"? without reaching any possibility of an answer. *Words fail us; we are often at a loss for words* when communicating around interculturality. Winnie's struggles dialogue directly with the experiences of interculturalists.

Bao, D. (2023). *Silence in English language pedagogy: From research to practice*. Cambridge University Press.

This book represents a precious entry into the topic of silence. Although it has to do with the specific context of English Language Pedagogy, the author offers very stimulating insights that can inspire us as 'communicators' around interculturality. Bao's use of poetry and visual arts to influence some thinking about the importance of silence cannot but inspire us to continue reflecting on its centrality for intercultural scholarship and education.

Notes

1 My translation of:

"Ensuite, j'ai trouvé aussi une autre citation. Je ne sais plus si elle vient de toi ni pourquoi elle est en allemand. Il semblerait que tu aies dit, à propos de Játékok: "Une sorte de mythologie du quotidien, une tentative pour apprivoiser les forces diaboliques de la vie de tous les jours". Est-ce possible que tu aies dit ça?
    GK: Ce n'est pas . . . pas impossible, aucune idée.
    Mais cette pensée ne t'est pas étrangère.
    GK: Non".

2 Borrowing Cage's timing in what follows, I suggest you take a short break to reflect on what I am saying in silence.

References

Angermuller, J. (2014). *Poststructuralist discourse analysis: Subjectivity in enunciative pragmatics*. Palgrave Macmillan.
Bakhtin, M. (1981). *The dialogic imagination: Four essays*. University of Texas Press.
Bao, D. (2023). *Silence in English language pedagogy: From research to practice*. Cambridge University Press.
Beckett, S. (2010). *Happy days*. Faber & Faber.
Blanchot, M. (1995). *The writing of the disaster*. University of Nebraska Press.
Brown, M. S., & O'Brien, D. (2020). The significance of silence. In M. Tian, F. Dervin, & G. Lu (Eds.), *Academic experiences of international students in Chinese higher education* (pp. 62–83). Routledge.
Burgess, C., Grice, C., & Wood, J. (2023). Leading by listening: Why aboriginal voices matter in creating a world worth living in. In K. E. Reimer, M. Kaukko, S. Windsor, K. Mahon, & S. Kemmis (Eds.), *Living well in a world living in for all* (pp. 115–136). Springer.
Caetano, A., Freire, I., & Machado, E. B. (2020). Student voice and participation in intercultural education. *Journal of New Approaches in Educational Research, 9*(1), 57–73.
Cage, J. (1961). *Silence: Lectures and writings*. Wesleyan University Press.
Cage, J. (2022). *4'33*. Alfred Music.
Cambridge Dictionary. (2023). *Voice*. https://dictionary.cambridge.org/dictionary/english/voice
Camus, A. (1970). *Lyrical and critical essays*. Vintage Books.
Camus, A. (1991). *The rebel*. Vintage Books.
Cocteau, J. (1930). *La Voix Humaine*. Librairie Stock.
Cohen, M. (2022). *The silence of the Miskito Prince: How cultural dialogue was colonized*. University of Minnesota Press.
Cook, C. (2023). *Autobiography*. https://catherinecookmezzo.com/performance-biography/
Dallmayr, F. (2003). *Dialogue among civilizations: Some exemplary voices*. Palgrave Macmillan.
Dervin, F. (2008). *Métamorphoses Identitaires en Situation de mobilité*. Turku University Press.
Dervin, F. (2016). *Interculturality in education*. Palgrave Macmillan.
Dervin, F. (2022). *Interculturality in fragments*. Springer.
Dervin, F. (2023). *The paradoxes of interculturality*. Routledge.
Ephratt, M. (2022). *Silence as language: Verbal silence as a means of expression*. Cambridge University Press.
Etymonline. (2023). *Voice*. www.etymonline.com/word/voice#etymonline_v_46523
Evans, J. (2017) Michel Leiris: Fibrils: The rules of the game, volume 3. *Translation and Literature 26*(3), 393–398.
Fleming, R. (2023). *L'expérience partagée de l'art change nos ondes cérébrales*. Interview. www.radiofrance.fr/franceculture/podcasts/affaires-culturelles/renee-fleming-est-l-invitee-d-affaires-culturelles-7961013
Freeden, M. (2022). *Concealed silences and inaudible*. Oxford University Press.

Gonzalez, A., & Chen, Y. W. (2015). *Our voices: Essays in culture, ethnicity, and communication*. Oxford University Press.

Ingoglia, S., Barrett, M., Iannello, N. M., Inguglia, C., Liga, F., Lo Cricchio, M. G., Tenenbaumn, H., Wiium, N., & Lo Coco, A. (2021). Promoting democratic and intercultural competences in the primary school context: The experience of "children's voices for a new human space". *Journal of Clinical and Developmental Psychology*, *3*(1), 45–57.

Jones, E. (Ed.). (2009). *Internationalization and the student voice*. Routledge.

Kurtag, G. (2009). *Entretiens, textes, dessins*. Editions Coontrechamps.

Leiris, M. (1997). *Scratches*. Johns Hopkins University Press.

Maldona, J., & Lazrus, L. (2019). A story of "rising voices" and intercultural collaboration. *Practicing Anthropology*, *41*(3), 34–37.

McDaniel, J. (1998). *Forgiveness parade*. Manic D Press.

Mudaly, R., & Sanjigadu, A. (2022). Epistemic journeying across abyssal lines of thinking: Towards reclaiming Southern voices. *Education as Change*, *26*(2), 2–29.

Nakane, I. (2017). *Silence in intercultural communication: Perceptions and performance*. John Benjamins.

Pascal, B. (2003). *Pensées*. Penguin.

Simpson, A., & Dervin, F. (2017). Democracy in education: An omnipresent yet distant other. *Palgrave Communications*, *3*(24). https://dx.doi.org/10.1057/s41599-017-0012-5

SISU. (2023). *Intercultural communication: Dynamics of cultural identities in global interaction (MOOC course)*. www.futurelearn.com/courses/intercultural-communication

Stanley, F. (2020). *Critical autoethnography and intercultural learning: Emerging voices*. Routledge.

Su, F., Wood, M., & Tribe, R. (2023). "Dare to be silent": Re-conceptualising silence as a positive pedagogical approach in schools. *Research in Education*, OnlineFirst. https://doi.org/10.1177/00345237231152604

Tubridy, D. (2010). Beckett, Feldman, Salcedo . . . neither. In D. Caselli (Ed.), *Beckett and nothing: Trying to understand Beckett* (pp. 143–159). Manchester University Press.

Voit, J. (2022). *Silence and its derivatives*. Palgrave Macmillan.

Wang, S., Moskal, M., & Schweisfurth, M. (2022). The social practice of silence in intercultural classrooms at a UK university. *Compare: A Journal of Comparative and International Education*, *52*(4), 600–617.

Yang, H. (2016). *A modernity set to a pre-modern tune: Classical-style poetry of modern Chinese writers*. Brill.

3 Scrutinizing

[Vocalizing]

1. The concept of ideology is omnipresent in this chapter and is positioned as central in the production, negotiation and dissemination of knowledge(s) about interculturality in education and research. What connotations and uses does this concept have in the literature that you have consulted, in your own work as a researcher and/or educator and in the socio-economic-political contexts you know?
2. Ideologies of interculturality compete with each other in the (often limited) acts of communication between researchers and educators. How often have you had the opportunity to confront others about your/their takes on interculturality? Which arguments have been at the core of these discussions? Has any new meaning, words or arguments emerged on such occasions?
3. Reflect for a moment on the centrality of language in communicating around interculturality. What aspects of language intervene in the (co-)production, (co-)negotiations, (co-)dissemination of knowledge around interculturality? Which aspects do you feel the most comfortable with?

Beyond a *passe-partout* approach?

1. Like millions of other people around the world, I have often stayed at a hotel. Until recently, I never really paid attention to the decoration, and especially to the works of art (paintings, prints) placed on the walls. A few months ago, I started observing the kind of art in the room I was going to occupy for a night in an international chain hotel. There were two pieces that were somewhat colourful while unflamboyant. The pieces were there, but they could have been removed without me noticing. At least, to me, they were insignificant, triggering no feelings of dis-/like. Other occupants might have liked them or felt strongly about them. One question then came to my mind: Why did the hotel choose these specific pieces for this room? What message(s) did they want to send to the customers (if any)? How did

they want to make the guests feel? I started speculating about the voices (to hint back at the previous chapter) that had engaged about these 'flavourless' pieces of art. Why was it that I felt this way about them? What in my own taste, previous artistic experiences and discussions with others had pushed me to not like them? I would like to compare this hotel experience to the way we are made to think about, appreciate, look down upon and engage around different versions of interculturality in research and education. While we feel nothing about some of these perspectives, others might appeal to us greatly. *Why is that?*

2. A *passe-partout* comes from French for *pass everywhere*. It refers to both a master key and a way of framing art, putting glass, cardboard, back of a frame and the art together. In this chapter, I deconstruct and argue against the passe-partout of interculturality, looking into the concepts of ideology, language and issues of translation, warning us about the illusions of 'sameness' and 'agreement' that we face when communicating around interculturality. As such, I propose to *scrutinize* the notion, using a verb that refers to *a search, an inquiry* in Latin, or, to be more precise, *a mode of election by ballot* that was used by the Church in Medieval Europe. Scrutiny is also related to the Proto-Indo-European root for *to cut* and *a cutting tool*. The Latin word might even have to do with *searching among rubbish (shreds)*. Looking into ideologies, language and translation, we cut through the polysemic and complex notion of interculturality that interests us in this book.

3. When we communicate around interculturality, bearing in mind the ideas of *voices* and *silences*, there are many layers of what I/we/you say/don't say that others don't have access to. As such, we often misinterpret, overinterpret, miss out, misuse and abuse each other's words. Nearly every week, I receive an email from one of my readers asking me to clarify what I have written. Here is an example with my answers to two questions they asked:

   Q: In one interview published in Chinese, you explain that "我的跨文化能力取决于语境，以及其他个体的存在。我的跨文化能力就是你的跨文化能力" (literal translation: *My Intercultural Competence is determined by the context and the presence of other individuals. My Intercultural Competence is also yours*). What was your intentional meaning? Could you explain it further in English?

   A: The interview you refer to was really badly translated in the article so half of what I said is easily misunderstandable. *My Intercultural Competence is determined by the context and the presence of other individuals. My Intercultural Competence is also yours* means that, in order to be 'interculturally competent' (whatever this might mean!), is always based on balancing acts with others. One cannot be 'competent' without others and vice versa. What others say and do always influences what we say and do – and vice versa. In the end no one really wins, no one really loses.

Q: Your book *Interculturality and the Political within Education* (Dervin & Simpson, 2021) explores interculturality in a critical and reflective perspective. When you argue that intercultural is always ideological and political, how can this help researchers, teachers and practitioners do interculturality free of the constraints of our own ideologies, nationalism or ethnocentrism? The elements behind culture you have emphasized in your work such as the economy and politics might be something too sensitive to talk or research, let alone the ideology itself as sort of taboo.

A: Yes, we all have these ideas in our heads (no choice, we are all 'brainwashed' one way or another). The idea is not to try to get rid of these elements (impossible) but by being aware of what they are and where they come from, we can try to expand our horizons by opening up to other such ideas. But basically, we cannot escape from all the phenomena that you list since we are always embedded in a specific economic-political context that forces us in-/directly to 'swallow' such ideas. We might reject them, however, depending on the power we have to speak and act, we are more or less free to shift to other ideologies. Ideologies are somewhat taboos that engulf us. I believe that individuals can reflect on them for themselves without necessarily involving others or voicing their disagreement. Ideologies are there to stay . . . We are only 'small things' in this world to act against them.

The questions from my interlocutor were mostly about reformulating and 'digging' deeper into what I had written by myself and/or with others in English, 'mediated' in another language ('bad' Chinese) in the first question. In the second question, the core of the issue is ideologies in the production of discourses around interculturality, which my interlocutor seems to 'reserve' for certain aspects and assertions about the notion – not realizing (maybe) that as soon as I/you/we open my/your/our mouth and 'state' anything about the notion, I/you/we cannot but fall into the realm of ideology, even in the most 'harmless', 'pseudo-objective' assertion about it. The choice of arguments, words, and even sentence structures, voices and silences, form together ideologemes (pieces of ideology). One cannot stand outside ideology for a 'scientific' construct like interculturality that has to do with the economy, politics, us, them, a given context versus another, the use of language to discuss it . . .

4. *We are all ideological beings.* In Roucek (1943, 1944), we are reminded rightly that the word ideology is polysemic, and yet, most of the definitions seem to have in common the idea that it corresponds to "a system of ideas generated by a few thinkers and subscribed to by large numbers" (Roucek, 1943, p. 39). Decisions made by any individual about their lives and thoughts are systematically based on (changing) convictions, which are grounded in such ideologies. In 'The war of ideologies' (1943)

Scrutinizing 39

Roucek positions ideologies as follows: The specific conceptual and discursive apparatus of an ideology constitutes the backbone 'in the architecture of our life'; ideologies present things as they 'ought to be' ('wishful thinking') rather than 'as they are', convincing us that "they tell the only and absolute 'truth', justifying and proving them right and unquestionable" (Roucek, 1943, p. 43); ideologies are both systems of thought and hidden forces, passed onto us through propaganda, education or coercion which might confuse assumptions with conclusions; ideologies evaluate and explain our experience rationally as well as "the future state of affairs for the improvement of society" (Roucek, 1943, p. 39); ideologies place boundaries in communication (what can/not be discussed by whom in specific contexts). Roucek (1943, p. 42) summarizes these points by arguing that ideologies "may be used as a means of [disguised] social control", disregarding and preventing people from questioning them (ideologies position other 'ideologies' as 'false'). [For Wisman (2023), following Marx, ideologies are even instruments of exploitation!]. Another important element found in Roucek's discussion of ideology (1944, p. 483), which we must bear in mind when reflecting on how we communicate around interculturality, is his argument that all discourses (including theories) "designed for social action, [are themselves] an ideology par excellence". Interculturality in research and education always has to do with 'social action'.

5. One important aspect of Roucek's take on ideology is central to reflecting on communicating around interculturality:

> Ideologies also automatically become the limits beyond which any debate may go. Arguments are permitted only within the framework of the ideology, and any attack on the ideology itself becomes a punishable heresy, since the faithful ones will tolerate no scepticism or criticism of the fundamentals. (Roucek, 1944, p. 45)

Communication can thus be easily short-circuited if one ideological take on a globally complex notion such as interculturality dominates and does not allow other takes to emerge, speak, debate and/or negotiate with its supporters. *Interculturality is about change. Interculturality is about revising who we are, what we do and what we think together.* The short-circuiting of the notion by ideological dominance is in direct contradiction with what interculturality wants from us. In a similar vein, Roucek (1943, p. 37) reminds us that as ideologists, we "hold[s] [our] theories as articles of faith; [we] habitually confuse [our] assumptions with [our] conclusions". This represents another major hurdle to communicating around interculturality, which needs to be put on the table, deconstructed and reconstructed again and again. Take the example of the ideology of *anti-culturalism*, which is based on good intentions, or the idea that *we should get rid of our stereotypes*. These are assumptions – we can be these; we must 'do' these interculturally – and yet many of us start with the conclusion that people are not doing it, arguing that they should do it. Following Roucek (1943, 1944), these assumptions become 'wishful thinking' rather than realistic and seriously achievable research and educational objectives. They fool us somehow into believing that we can become *superhumans* without any 'bad thoughts' or 'stereotypes', free from economic-political influences.

6. Let us explore a short and interesting example of how ideology pervades the way we might engage with interculturality. The example is taken from the global US-centric entertainment industry. The American singer Gwen Stefani was once accused of cultural appropriation (see Rowell, 1995) towards an aspect of 'Japanese culture' (so-called Harajuku culture related to a specific district of Tokyo). In her remarks about this period in her career, the singer said: "I think it was a beautiful time of creativity . . . a time of the ping-pong match between Harajuku culture and American culture. If we didn't buy and sell and trade our cultures in, we wouldn't have so much beauty, you know" (NBC News, 2023). Interestingly, she does not seem to shy away from a dominant ideology of today's 'cannibal capitalism' (Fraser, 2022): the market economy. For the singer, 'borrowing' from Japan and mixing with 'American culture' was about profit-making while 'creating beauty'. In many arguments in our communication around interculturality as scholars and educators, I often feel that we share similar views, in more or less open ways. I am thinking here of the many conversations I have had with scholars who justified their use of a specific model of intercultural competence or of an ideologeme by mentioning that these open the doors to publication and access to 'dominant' and 'dominating' voices, often to be used for one's own benefit (promotion, local fame . . .). I have worked with scholars who see no problem in 'co-publishing' with me, following my own ideological takes, while including at the same time in their own teaching and 'research' (which has turned out to be mere endorsement for governments in some cases), 'famous' American multiculturalists or Canadian psychologists whose ideologies represent clear clashes with what I had been writing with/for them. The contradictory accumulation of ideological takes is 'normal' somehow whenever we address the issue of interculturality. Yet this accumulation needs to be discussed in the open and be ethically evaluated against cannibalistic capitalism – willingly using ideologies as a way of 'enriching oneself' and/or 'getting personal benefits' needs to be identified and questioned.
7. A list of questions around ideology, capitalism and communication around interculturality then comes to mind: Why is it that we cannot always communicate around interculturality in research and education? Who is (not) given the floor to speak? Whose ideologies seem to dominate in a given space and time? Why? Who tells us that we cannot communicate around

interculturality in certain ways and why? How much are we coerced into illusions of communication? Why don't we feel that we are (really) communicating around the notion at moment X? How much is the issue of 'money' openly/implicitly included in the way we communicate around interculturality? What ideological positions reveal its inclusion/hidden presence?

8. The concept of ideology has been used in analyzing discourses of culture (e.g., LaCapra, 1988) before it became a minor concept in research on interculturality. In one of the first papers to use ideology as an analytical framework in relation to intercultural communication, Kim (2007) explores how the central concept of cultural identity is dealt with by means of the ideologies of, e.g., assimilationism, pluralism, integrationism, and separatism in research on interculturality. Holmes et al. (2018) place the expression of 'intercultural dialogue' within the framework of the ideology of the European Union, criticizing the illusions that it might create in interpreting how people meet interculturally. Phipps (2014, p. 112) argues rightly that "intercultural dialogue is inoperable and problematic under the present conditions of globalisation and migration, where there exists conflict, vulnerability, and instability". In a 2020 article, Verkuyten, Yogeeswaran, Mepham and Sprong label interculturalism as a 'new diversity ideology' based on dialogue, unity and identity flexibility. The authors argue that it differs from multiculturalism and can 'improve' intergroup relations . . . (which is a good example of ideologism in itself!). Holliday (2010) placed ideology at the centre of the stage with his important book entitled *Intercultural Communication and Ideology*, which represented a direct blow to the dominating ideology of culturalism and essentialism at the time – while at the same time reinvesting the now well-rehearsed ideology of non-culturalism, contributing to the puerile battles of words between 'essentialists' and 'non-essentialists'. In recent years, my own work (Dervin, 2022, 2023) and my cooperation with Simpson (Dervin & Simpson, 2021) and Jacobsson (Dervin & Jacobsson, 2022) have also placed ideology at the centre of interculturality work in education and communication studies. We have examined and analyzed how supranational institutions such as the Council of Europe and the OECD impose specific (Western-centric and capitalist) ideologies, in cooperation with dominating scholars, to the rest of the world, often claiming to be doing 'global', 'sustainable' and 'democratic' work. In my latest publications (Dervin, 2022), I have delved into the in-/direct ideological manipulation of discourses on interculturality through the misuse of (translated) words – we shall come back to this in the next section. In his 2023 article entitled *The affective ideology of the OECD global competence framework: implications for intercultural communication education* Zembylas (2023) follows a similar path by focusing on how affect is used ideologically in the preparation of students for interculturality.

9. What differences do we need to make between, e.g., *theory, epistemology* and *ideology* when we communicate around interculturality? Is the abuse of the word *theory*, which tends to mean nothing and everything at the same time, a way of hiding our own ideologism(s)? How many (inconvenient) voices are silenced (e.g., by reviewers) in the name of 'theory' versus 'ideology' while we might all be mere ideologists when it comes to interculturality? Remembering Orwell (2001, p. 167), we might want to pay further attention to his words when communicating (reading, writing, listening, speaking) with others:

> At any given moment there is an orthodoxy, a body of ideas which it is assumed that all right-thinking people will accept without question. It is not exactly forbidden to say this, that or the other, but it is 'not done' to say it, just as in mid-Victorian times it was 'not done' to mention trousers in the presence of a lady. Anyone who challenges the prevailing orthodoxy finds himself silenced with surprising effectiveness.

As scholars and educators, as much as we must be aware of this orthodoxy, we have a mission to fight against it and to free a lot of space for heterodoxies . . .

10. A simple look at a list of references used in a book/an article (which indicates acts of communication in the process of writing somehow) can reveal how ideologies and capitalism are distributed and dominate the kind of communication that an author wishes to project. What languages are included? Which economic-political contexts? Whose dominating/marginal voices? What silences? Etc.
11. For Wittgenstein (1975, p. 22): "But doesn't it come out here that knowledge is related to a decision?" One cannot talk about and (refuse to) negotiate around interculturality without being ideological, without being influenced by broader economic-political discourses in our decisions to define, problematize and 'do' interculturality in specific ways, without giving *orders* about what one should do about/with the notion, and, at the same time, without pushing forth (hidden) representations and agendas concerning who we (are made to believe we) are. We decide how we (co-)construct and thus communicate knowledge around interculturality based on these complex processes that often dominate us without realizing it.
12. The ways we engage and communicate around interculturality change with time and space, navigating back to previous ideological spheres that we might have privileged, rejected and criticized negatively in our earlier lecturing and writing. *Ideologies come and go. Ideologies appear when they are not meant to be there. Ideologies might find their way in what we say because we miscommunicate with others or because things might get mistranslated and misconstrued.* We prefer to use certain ideologemes at moment X (e.g., democracy) and others at moment Y (e.g., tolerance).

Recently, one of my Ph.D. researchers started writing his 'intellectual autobiography' in relation to interculturality. The way he started to construct it seemed to indicate a 'positive' trend, with his recent engagement around the notion through anti-essentialism deemed 'better' than his culturalist phase. Often, we might feel, like this young researcher, that we have 'evolved' and that we have become better at researching and/or educating for interculturality. However, I believe that this is an illusion. As such, the boundaries between the complex ideological worlds that we need to cross constantly when dealing with interculturality are not so clear-cut. An ideological position such as culturalism (which places culture at the centre of everything we say and do, see Holliday, 2010) or anti-culturalism does not necessarily remain static, and I/you/we can easily find myself/yourself/ourselves jumping from one ideology to another – sometimes even without realizing. Since anti-culturalism (and anti-essentialism, for that matter) cannot be 'practised' fully, dipping back into other ideologies of interculturality is 'normal', even when we try hard not to appear 'culturalist' or 'essentialist'. One important aspect of communicating around interculturality is that we do not have access to what is happening outside our own sphere of interaction. *What we say and do does not necessarily correspond to what we think about what we say and do and/or should say and do.* In interactions with others, we often hide our feelings, our 'real' thoughts; we camouflage our inner contradictions and incoherencies; we put 'accepted' ideologies on the table without being convinced; we say white while we mean black; we agree with others (because of power relations) while we disagree inside us; etc.

13. What an ideology perspective in the communication around interculturality tells us is that we are always limited in the ways we discuss, problematize, renegotiate, define and analyze such a complex and polysemic notion. We speak and write about it, and yet we can never really reach the complexities of the notion. For Barthes (1978), speaking or discoursing does not correspond to communicating but 'enslaving' self and others. We are enslaved by the multiple inner and outer voices and silences that contribute to our ideological co-construction of the notion. I am thinking here of the art exhibition of an Iranian artist that I visited in 2022. I was attracted by the piece of art reproduced on the exhibition poster. It looked somehow 'special'. As soon as I entered the hall, I was struck by what I perceived to be a 'clash' between the exciting pieces and the texts that had been written for each of them. As I started reading the English text, I realized that the discourses about the pieces sounded very 'U.S.-centric'. I could not relate what I saw (as special and original) in the art pieces and the very ideological takes on, e.g., 'gender', 'social justice' and 'community' used in English. The art and the accompanying texts seemed to come from different worlds, from different ideological universes somehow. As I read more about the artist, I realized that he

was born in Iran but had moved to the U.S. in his twenties and studied at a famous U.S. university. It was extraordinary to note that, while the art took me to other ideological worlds, the text was a standard rendition of dominating ideological takes on the aforementioned issues – as if they had been copied and pasted from other sources. This ideological clash needs to be paid attention to in research and education, too. As such, I often feel that the way research is done in some countries reproduces this clash: the context starts to blend in and be dominated by ideological takes (e.g., in the use of specific ideologemes), which negates somehow the specificities and complexities of other ideological domains. One example might be the exclusive use of U.S.-centric perspectives on multicultural education (which cannot but relate to the economic-political context of the U.S.) to examine Chinese Minzu 'minority' education in the English language.

14. Let me finish this section on ideologies of interculturality by mentioning a few persistent ideologies and ideologisms that deserve to be identified, deconstructed and communicated around so that we might expand our ideological takes on the notion. They are presented in alphabetical order:

(the) Belief in intercultural effectiveness
(the) Centrality of culture to 'govern' intercultural relations
Contact hypothesis
Culture shock
Democratic culture
(the) Dichotomy of *intra-* and *inter-cultural*
(the) Fear of failure
Intercultural competence
Interculturality as a unitary concept ('the intercultural approach')
Interculturality as a problem
Interculturality is a new phenomenon
Interculturality is neutral and has nothing to do with politics
Interculturality is something that can be learnt
(the) Need to approach interculturality objectively in research and education
Our world is becoming more diverse . . .
Steps in intercultural competence
Stereotypes can be removed
Some people are better than others at interculturality
Success as a must in interculturality

Persistent ideologisms include: *Culturalism, essentialism, integrationism, social justicism, but also Banksism, Byramism (intercultural citizenshipism), Dervinism (Baumanian liquidism), Hofstedeism, Hollidayism (small culturism), Pillerism* . . .

Languaging interculturality

On two occasions, Aesop was asked by his master to organize a feast with the best food he could find. He decided to serve tongues, cooked and seasoned in different ways. Noticing the disappointment and disgust of his own guests, his Master asked Aesop: "Did I not tell you, sirrah, to provide the choicest dainties that money could procure?" The slave replied: "And what excels the Tongue?", arguing that the tongue leads to learning and philosophy – to which everyone in the dining hall applauded. Aesop added: "Treasons, violence, injustice, and fraud are debated, resolved upon, and communicated by the Tongue. It is the ruin of empires, cities, and of private friendships" (Aesop, 2023).

In this section, we focus on the role of language in communicating around interculturality, discussing the importance of translation.

I use the neologism of *languaging* to reflect on the instabilities and ideological uses imposed by language (see Dervin & Jacobsson, 2021).

In trying to communicate around interculturality, we face what I would refer to as a puzzling contradiction: we keep insisting on the importance of language and trans-languaging, and yet when we do research and write about interculturality, we tend to forget about language – that 'tool' of communication that we often feel does not deserve our full attention.

I argue here that all engagement with interculturality must be critical of language to 'revise' communication and to add to some of the rare calls for a languaging turn in communication around interculturality (see Holmes et al., 2022).

Let's look at interculturality through the omnipresent and yet often invisible lens of language.

Language is never straightforward – even and especially in research where the ideologies of rationality and objectivity blind us in front of this important aspect of communicating.

For Gordin (2015, p. 23) "The scholarship you read is always biased by the linguistic capacities of the scholar. It's only honest to admit it".

My linguistic world is, in fact, very limited since I only operate and navigate through some Indo-European and Finno-Ugric languages.

Many worlds are closed to my take on interculturality; I cannot open their door and even peek inside what they say and do about the notion because of my limited language skills.

I can never be sure that what I communicate around interculturality will be understood by others – or understood in ways that somehow relate to what I am trying to say.

This awareness is also a violent reminder of who we are as human beings.

Wittgenstein (1975, p. 49) tells us: "What is the proof that I know something? Most certainly not my saying I know it".

Language enslaves us in the way we communicate around interculturality; I listen to myself and to others, and I feel that I am ensnared in bubbles; I often feel that I can hear, but I cannot expand my listening experiences to other ideological spheres – language forces me to say things I am not necessarily in control of, with extra layers of connotations and meanings depending on the interlocutor.

In using the dominating, imperialistic, discriminatory and (financially) power-laden academic lingua franca of today (see a 'classic', Skutnabb-Kangas & Robertson, 1995), we run the risk of not communicating at all if we merely assume that using words as they stand in a monolingual or bilingual dictionary will suffice. Bellos (2012, p. 82) reminds us that:

> It's an indisputable fact about languages that the sets of words that each possesses divide up the features of the world in slightly and sometimes radically different ways. Colour terms never match up completely, and it's always a problem for a French speaker to know what an English person means by 'brown shoes', since the footwear in question may be marron, bordeaux, even rouge foncé. The names of fishes and birds often come in non-matching sets of labyrinthine complexity; similarly, fixed formulae for signing off letters come in graded levels of politeness and servility that have no possible application outside of the culture in which they exist.

We need to be careful not to fall into the trap of mere differentialism *only*. Languages differ but also overlap in what they allow us (not) to do.

However, Bellos (2012) sends us an important message here for communicating around interculturality: a word should never be assumed to be a 'mere' equivalent of another since every word used to communicate around interculturality in education and research cannot but be 'coloured' by the economic-political, the ideological and globalized languaging preferences.

I remember angering a crowd of scholars and educators in France some years ago when I used the word 'race' in French to ask the question of racism in intercultural scholarship. One scholar got very emotional and told me that I could not use this word in France because race did not exist. I tried to problematize the idea of racism further, asking the audience what it was about, beyond the socially constructed idea of race.

AI, e.g., through ChatGPT, can now 'express' things for us humans. Recently, a friend sent me what an AI tool had produced to create my own biodata. It said:

> Fred Dervin is a French-Finnish sociologist, professor, and author who has written extensively on issues of ethnic identity, globalization, and internationalism. He is the director of the Research Project on Transnational/Transcultural Exchange in Youth Cultures at the University of Helsinki.

Reading through these words, the way ChatGPT had 'languaged me', produced by an artificial 'stranger', I felt somehow alienated. All these words are understandable and somehow contain some truth, but reading through the sentences, I don't see myself since I don't feel that these words faithfully represent my work (e.g., I never talk about *ethnic identity*; I was never the director of the mentioned project, etc.). Although these words look 'beautiful' somehow, they are not *me*.

Barthes (2020) places our relationships with language within the continuum of *anguish* and *jouissance-pleasure* – when we communicate around interculturality, we navigate between these two poles, experiencing contradictory emotions with others, openly and inside us.

I hear what an institution has to say about its internationalization; I hear what I have heard elsewhere; I hear good intentions, unclear terms, unrealistic goals; more importantly, I hear repeated, recycled words and ideologies; I don't hear just one voice but many voices in these statements – with some incomprehensible or unknown to me.

Cocteau (2013, p. 63) says: "Beyond the fact that words have meaning, they are endowed with a magical virtue, a spell-binding power, a hypnotic quality, a fluid that works apart from the meaning they possess".

A lot of what I/you/we say about interculturality is on the verge of the stereotype, this solid linguistic form and voice that repeats itself like a basic robot.

My own words about interculturality are maybe rarely 'mine'.

My words don't belong to me but (selectively) to the whole world and to others (too).

Since academia is about authority and legitimacy (one must earn the right to speak in a publication or in a lecture), it is deemed essential to control how one communicates.

I repeat what others say; marking the distance between us at times (*as XX says*), and yet, often, I merely parrot without realizing it.

Others' words and formulae have become part of my voice; at times, I activate language for interculturality like a tightrope walker, ensuring that I don't say the wrong things to the wrong people at the wrong time – thus self-censoring our act of communication.

In his work on language, Barthes (1989) sees two types of language that can help us think further about the options to expand our takes on communicating around interculturality: *encratic languages,* which have to do with ideologies and relate to state, institutional and ideological apparels, and *acratic languages,* which aim to go beyond official, power-laden discourses.

Encratic languages are "vague" (Barthes, 1989) and correspond to the languages of the *doxa* and *vox populi* – these unidentifiable voices spread through, e.g., social media today (see previous chapter).

Encratic languages often win over since they are omnipresent and often supported by the powers that be.

Acratic languages try to delink from these voices by questioning them and how they function.

When he wrote about these languages, Barthes (1989) believed that Marxist discourse, structuralism and psychoanalysis were examples of acratic languages.

Today no language appears to be suited to stand within the acratic sphere.

Any way of positioning, defining, problematizing and communicating around interculturality is encratic willy-nilly.

There is a need to move away from the idea/illusion that words will explain and present what interculturality is about and entails in 'proper', 'adequate' and 'competent' ways.

Communicating around interculturality bears a big responsibility, especially if I speak over and for others; speaking too much and in ways that do not reflect their own experiences and feelings might be detrimental to others.

Who cares about language?

Before moving on to the central and vital issue of translation, based on a limited number of recently published papers in an important journal (*Language and Intercultural Communication*), I discuss how issues of language and languaging are treated. I picked the four first research articles published in volume 22, issue 6 of 2022 since this is not meant to be exhaustive but exploratory. I could have chosen any other journal related to interculturality to have a close look at language and languaging, but this specific journal (for which I have a lot of respect) lays the emphasis on language in its title. While reading these papers, focusing on their 'meta-take' on language issues, I was often reminded of how much I have neglected many of the aspects described in what follows.

The first article is based on data collected in Dutch with 'migrants' (I place the word between inverted commas since it is a very polysemic term around the world – the authors do not problematize it in the paper). English translations accompany the Dutch originals, but no explanations or justifications are provided as to why the authors decided to translate the data as is. The methodological section only refers to the way the discursive analysis was performed (pronominal usage, lexical choices). The analysis is discursive (only) and relies somehow on the English translation of the data. If we do not speak Dutch, i.e., if we don't know the specificities of the language in terms of pronominal usage, could we be (unintentionally) misled?

The second article deals with American uploaders' success in a Chinese video-sharing website and focuses on transnational identity. The authors make use of Darvin and Norton's (2015) sociocultural linguistic construct of identity and investment. References to language are made in passing, e.g., to the Chinese words for *microcelebrities* (wanghong, 网红) and *property management company* (物管) in one of the microbloggers' videos, in passing but not

Scrutinizing 49

detailed or problematized. The translation appears to be obvious in the article and 'McDonaldized' in the sense that the hundreds of multilingual readers of the journal may picture different realities and connotations in seeing what appears to be 'mere dictionary forms' in the translated data. The authors do comment on the study participants' own use of language, and yet they never reflect back on their own use of both Chinese and English in the construction of their academic writing.

The third article has to do with the multimodal construction of interculturality in YouTube videos and is based on data produced in the Chinese language. However, in the entirety of the article, only an unproblematized English translation of two YouTube videos is used. The author asserts that they take into account the participants' dynamic and flexible multilingual practices. But, when language is unproblematized about English translations of the research data, how much of this dynamism and flexibility are we missing as readers? It is noteworthy though, that the author does discuss their own language skills:

> Adopting a postmodern interpretation requires the researcher to acknowledge one's role in the shaping of data and the co-construction of meaning. The researcher in this case is a multilingual speaker of Cantonese, Mandarin, and English, and has been residing in the East Asia region when the pandemic broke out. It is from this vantage point that the data is interpreted and made sense of. My knowledge of the US context came from the media, and my reading of academic articles which introduced me to the multiculturalism and multilingualism in the US.
>
> (Ho, 2022, p. 664)

Yet, *languaging stops here*. The article contains no comment on word choice from the researcher's perspective, no comment on translation (with discussions of problems faced) and no self-reflexivity concerning own use of language. Again, as if the scholar's language was clear-cut and transparent.

Article four is conceptual and deals with translanguaging creativity, using Michel de Certeau's ideas as a counterpoint to current thinking in global (English-based) research on translanguaging. It is noteworthy that the paper does not engage with translanguaging as a complex reality for scholars themselves *at all*. Again, the impression is that language is an issue about those we work upon and study (maybe educate too?) but not about 'us' – the scholar is 'evacuated'!

[The *inter-* of interculturality concerns the scholar, too, and especially the scholar commenting on the other . . . who is at their mercy.]

The final article deals with the important issue of Indigenous education in Australia. It looks into issues of language policy and practice. Again, the paper represents a good defense of 'diversity' and 'multilingualism' in education. The authors explain:

> The paper argues that the failure to provide quality education to remote and very remote Indigenous students is a product of both racism and neoliberalism. Neoliberalism refers to the application of business modes of management in social sectors that have traditionally not experienced this. The resulting economic market rationale displaces education goals of equity and democratic citizenship.

Disappointingly, nothing is said of the position, role and responsibility of the one(s) writing and reporting about these issues. The writer's and scholar's own ways of ideologizing through words must also be opened up. Why is this nearly systematically missing from our work? The five articles discussed briefly here do talk about language but without really looking at its own functioning in their own mirror. How much does the way we miss out on languaging around the data, word choice and translation disturb and distract in the way we communicate around interculturality? Thompson and Dooley (2019, p. 63) note:

> In multilingual research, translation procedures are crucial; inadequately translated tools and data can lead to invalid conclusions. Furthermore, when translation procedures are unclear or unstated, the trustworthiness and replicability of the research are compromised.

Some readers might feel that I am 'dancing on the head of a pin'. However, I want us to understand and accept that these elements are not mere details but that they are central in methodological, epistemic and ethical terms in the way we do research and communicate in research and education. Language has several functions, as we have seen in an earlier section – neglecting any of these functions cannot but disturb research, education and the intricate realities of interculturality.

Translation as 'normal' breathing?

> "I just enjoy translating, it's like opening one's mouth and hearing someone else's voice emerge".
>
> Murdoch (2014, p. 48)

[In the language of Ancient Babylon, *translator* meant a 'language tuner'. As someone constantly working on interculturality in different (European) languages and in contact with Chinese, I need to 'tune in' most of what others and I say in my head – often without realizing – reengaging with our words *again and again*.]

[For as long as I can remember, translation has been with me, one way or another, knowingly or subconsciously, every day of my life. Translation was a daily (tedious) task at school (English, French, German, Greek, Latin) during my childhood. In Latin, teaching-learning revolved exclusively around translating together with the teacher what we called the 'Bible' – a massive volume of classics. For the weekly tests, we would learn the translations by heart and regurgitate them. In the French language, we did what was referred to as *thème* and *version* (translating from and into another language). At home, translation was constantly happening in my head and between family members, friends and acquaintances. We also mixed languages in informal situations, trespassing the usual process of translation to complexify it – no need to translate when we (believe we) all understand the languages that we are using. One of my uncles taught me to be curious about translation at a young age and made a habit of having me translate and check texts on food packages while cooking, to "keep your linguistic mind busy and not waste your time" – *this is still with me today*. Translation has always been omnipresent, but, in most cases, I don't realize that it is *here and there*. I was, in fact, destined to be a translator and/or an interpreter – two different 'professions' that many of us amalgamate. While we were discussing our future career plans with a group of close friends and their parents at the age of 12, one parent told me: "You must work at the UN. You were born to be a translator". (All my friends were to become high-ranking civil servants, doctors or lawyers; I am the only professor.) I never thought of translation and/or interpreting as a 'job' but as *facts of life*. I tried them as a profession, but I did not enjoy them a single minute. I was, in fact, never good at translating/interpreting, I think. I have always felt that my 'professional' translation and interpreting were like hyperventilation – forcing myself to breathe harder on paper or in a microphone. *Translation should be 'normal' breathing, I feel*.]

[Strangely enough, in the 25 years that I have been involved in intercultural research and education, I have had very few (formal) conversations around translation with colleagues, students and/or educators. Obviously, like all interculturalists, translation has been part of my practice and thinking, but it has been rarely voiced. When I worked in a department of linguistics, translation was (maybe) a bit more visible, although we seemed to make a clear division between us '(applied) linguists' and them 'translation specialists'. While some of the 'translators' were easily navigating between translation studies and other subfields of linguistics, probably because of their need to survive as a field that was in danger of disappearing (not 'research-focused' enough for a Finnish university), crossing over from linguistics to translation was neither common nor considered somehow. When I shifted towards 'education sciences' in the 2010s, I discovered the voice of translation to be entirely muted. I realized then that something was very wrong. When one of my first Ph.D. students in education sent me a first draft of their research paper, I remember being horrified by the fact that they had included only a (bad, obviously AI-based) translation in English of data they had collected in the Finnish language. *No comment on the process of translating the data, no sign of the original language, which was relegated to the position of a ghost, and no discussion of the influence of translation processes on both the analysis and ethics.* I wrote them an email straight away, raising my concerns and asking for clarifications. For not including the originals and discussions of how translation took place, the student explained that "space is limited, I am already above the authorized word count" . . . I repeat this frightening phrase: *authorized word count*. Translation was discarded, deemed superfluous or even 'useless' because of restrictions, which in the end have to do with financial (word count relates to the number of pages printed and edited) and 'administrative-scientific' reasons (translation is rarely used as a criterion to decide if a paper could be published). After noticing this conundrum repeatedly with new Ph.D. students, I made it compulsory to both reflect on and take openly into account the issue of translation. The lack of awareness and interest in 'language' issues in research on interculturality that I notice with many students is something that we need to address urgently. Language and translation are not just reserved for 'language people' (applied linguists, language educators . . .), it matters for all of us.]

[In a similar vein, when I read and review research papers based on multilingual data, I rarely hear the complex voices of the participants, which appear to be drowned under other voices, mostly that of the researcher(s)-writer(s). *Faulty snapshots of the participants' voices.* I *overhear* the participants somehow (like putting one's head under water, one hears sounds), but I know that what I hear is somewhat limited, fragmentary, and even incorrect and manipulated since we are rarely told how these voices have been 'transferred' onto paper. Discussions of translation are absent as if what we make others say in another language was 'obvious', 'natural' or 'simply moved from one place to another'. I often feel that we keep mistreating languages and thus translation in research and education, even many of those whose focus is directly on language and intercultural communication. Language is seen as an object but is not considered the main substance of what we do when we speak and write about interculturality as a subject of research and education (see Holmes et al., 2022 about what they call 'the politics of researching multilingually'). My work with Chinese colleagues (Mainland China) has also added another layer of awareness of the importance of translating *alone* and *together with* others. When we started cooperating, we rarely discussed the words that we used in English as a Lingua Franca – the language we used to publish together. We never reflected on what I have come to call the 'flavours' of words. Since they tended to be very polite in front of a 'famous white man' (!), my own flavours systematically 'won over' until the day I started to suspect that what we were doing was probably as problematic as what I had noticed in some of my students, colleagues and myself in other contexts. So, we began to deconstruct and renegotiate the words we used to assemble theoretical frameworks, data analyses and transcriptions of data. We found our conversations around translation to be highly time-consuming but very rewarding and indispensable to propose a revised version of interculturality beyond my former highly Eurocentric work. We thus made a habit of discussing translations since we realized that a much longer process of negotiation is indeed needed. I have reviewed some of these discussions in publications post-2020 (Dervin & Simpson, 2021; Dervin & Yuan, 2022; Dervin & R'boul, 2022; Dervin, 2022).]

Reloading translation for interculturality

[Translation is not just a matter of words but, most importantly, of communication and negotiations and co-constructions. This is why every single interculturalist must don their translator masks as often as possible, even when they are assumed to work in just one language.]

[We must care about translation as much as we care about (randomly) 'culture', 'identity', 'rationality', 'post-. . .', 'ethics', 'social justice' . . . as interculturalists. We must include it, problematize it, renegotiate and revise it; we must admit to its failures and successes. Translation should not just be a mere footnote in research papers and books. To me, ignoring the intricacies of translation is producing 'poor' interculturality in research and education.]

[The story and legend of *Yu Boya and Zhong Ziqi* from the Spring and Autumn Period (770–476 B.C.E.) or the Warring States Period (475–221 B.C.E.) allows me to problematize this further. Yu Boya, a historical household name for qin playing (the Chinese 'plucked zither'), was playing his instrument one day when he felt that someone was listening to him, a woodcutter who was enjoying and being sensitive to his music. He played many of his tunes to the man and noticed that he could feel what the pieces were about. For example, when high mountains were described, the woodcutter would comment on the connections between the characteristics of Boya's music and the mountains. This all left Boya ecstatic since this was the first time that someone had really appreciated and made sense of what he was trying to convey through his musical language. Boya and Ziqi became bosom friends and, in Chinese, 知音 (zhiyin) came to signify *knowing the tone, a friend keenly appreciative of one's talents* and even *an intimate/bosom friend*. The legend became part of the Chinese National Intangible Cultural Heritage in 2014. This somehow symbolizes my dream of and proposal for translational relations in intercultural research and education. *We should feel translation together* – scholars/scholars, scholars/research participants, educators/students . . . We should become *translational bosom friends*. I argue that translation is about balancing, again and again, the evolving and necessarily negotiable meanings and connotations of words and discourses together with others.]

[*Traduction*, 翻译, *käännös, översättning, übersetzung, þýðing*. In Finnish *to translate* can be either *kääntää* or *suomentaa*: *to turn* and *to make Finnish*. The Latin word behind the word translation in English also hints at the action of turning.]

[Although in research today, specific forms of *trans-* are highly popular (*trans*-languaging and *trans*-cultural increasingly), the *trans-* of translation, which relates to the verb *transfer* and *the action of carrying across, transporting* from Latin, seems unappealing somehow. Because of its long history and the fact that most of us might not have had such positive experiences with the act of translating at school, I assume that the word *translation* could sound too 'dry', too 'old-fashioned' and, somehow, for many, too 'traumatic' to be deemed 'usable' in intercultural research and education. In other words, translation often appears to have very little appeal for interculturalists. (I am hoping that I might be generalizing here.) When I see the very word *translation* in the different languages above, I realize that these words sound different to me and probably to the readers who can speak these languages. Reflecting on what feelings and emotions, but also ideologies and representations one might experience when hearing the word *translation* in English and other languages, is a first necessary step in revising our convictions (and/or lack of) that translation plays a central role in interculturality work. This is what I call *reloading translation for interculturality*.]

[Navigating through the 'classics' of interculturality published in English over the past decades from Hofstede et al. (2010) to Byram (1997), Holliday (2010) to Piller (2011) (and also my own work, e.g., see Dervin, 2016), and the five articles discussed in the previous section, the absence of translation as a serious and central aspect of scholarship and education takes the wind out of our sails. It is never named, never problematized, never argued for in the way we 'do' things scientifically, methodologically, discursively and ideologically. The use of knowledge from different geo-economic-political-linguistic spheres occurs 'Englishingly' ('naturally'?), hiding away the complexities that it contains in hundreds of different languages. The fact that all these books rely solely on the English language seems to disenfranchise us from 'caring' about translation or even treating English itself as a complex source of pluralities (*Englishes* rather than the English language). Things appear to be crystallized as 'obvious', 'taken for granted' as if the authors were saying *I write in English, a universal monolithic language understood by all* [an illusion!], *so there is no need to translate anything or reflect on what the words I use might mean to you as a speaker of other Englishes and languages*. The English language is a fantastic mediator, but it needs to be pluralized and interculturalized to ensure that all kinds of speakers get heard and listened to beyond the illusion of monolingualism. Translation, I believe, has a central role to play for interculturalists here.]

[I need to take a short break here to remind my readers that the idea of translating something, although it might be associated with positive 'rosy' phenomena such as allowing access to a good book or a film as signs of hospitality or even empathy, has also had to do with pain, fear, horror and violence. For example, how would you feel if you had to translate the book of a tyrant such as Hitler? Translation has also been used for war, country annexation, destruction and colonization (see Samoyault, 2020). I note that the artist Kenneth Goldsmith (2016) has problematized this rarely discussed aspect of translation in a small book called *Against Translation* (published in Arabic, Chinese, English, French, German, Japanese and Russian) in which he discusses the impasses and shortcomings of translation and calls the process of translating 'obsolescent' in our times since it cannot deal with the fluidity that we experience on a daily basis.]

[The act of translating is very much anchored in the kind of world we live in today and reflects the pressure and feelings that we experience. As such, translation is also about power. Translation is political and ideological. I/you/we may have the power *to be entitled* to translate something for all/ specific individuals; the power to decide how to (not) translate something; the power to mistranslate strategically to manipulate and simplify (see the abuse of the translation of the word snow in the so-called 'Eskimo' language which has been used in communicating around interculturality for decades, Pullum, 1991); translation is also part of today's cannibal capitalism (Fraser, 2022). In academia, since every word counts in, e.g., research articles, one might decide not to include original utterances from research participants to save words (and thus 'money').]

[The work of Juliane House and Dániel Z. Kádár (with some Chinese colleagues) is fascinating for problematizing translation and interculturality. In their 2022 article entitled *The problem of translating Chinese policy related expressions: a case study of wenming ('civilised')* (House et al., 2022), they tackle a word that has always fascinated me in the Chinese language, 文明, which is omnipresent in the Mainland, especially in governmental policies and information (Dervin et al., 2022). In the paper, they review the difficulties of translating the word – which might appear simple at first, *civilization*. However, the very word has manifold meanings and uses and is a clearly 'linguaculturally embedded' expression. For example, in Figure 3.1., the two sets of Chinese characters, containing the word *wenming* and another word which translates word-for-word in English as *Civility/civilization and courtesy*, are translated as *Be polite and friendly* – *wenming* here referring to politeness. In order to translate the term in 'equivalent ways', House et al. (2022) use a contrastive pragmatic approach that goes well beyond the mere dictionary meanings of expressions. They recognize that signs of subjectivity in the choice of translation is inevitable. I add that this subjectivity needs to be emphasized by researchers and spelt out. That the word 文明 does not just translate as 'civilized' in English is an important reminder to scholars and

56 Scrutinizing

Figure 3.1 Sign at a café in China containing the characters for *civility/civilization/civilized* and *courtesy*

educators communicating around interculturality that any 'interlingual' element needs to be unpacked and discussed with others for both the sake of transparency and fairness.]

[In *The American Rhythm*, for instance, Austin (2007) uses the idea of *re-expressions* to refer to translations of Amerindian songs.]

Betraying

[Most readers will have come across the Italian saying *Traduttore, traditore*, which translates as *translator, traitor* (i.e., *the translator is a traitor*), hinting at the impossibility of translating *fully – in other words:* translating can never be 'perfect'. This paronomasia (use of words that sound similar but differ in meanings) could discourage many of us who live with and through translating. *We are all traitors linguistically*. However, in this book, I claim that betraying is unavoidable and necessary in intercultural research and education and that we need to both accept and deal with this fact of life. *What do I mean by this?* I wish to twist the Italian saying by turning betraying into a motivating and stimulating force. As much as interculturality is a never-ending process (see the suffix *-ality*), translation must urge us to enter into multiple, multilayered and endless dialogues with all those involved in our research and education activities: from the colleagues we read and borrow from in different languages to the migrant worker we have interviewed in Inner Mongolia with whom we must deconstruct, renegotiate and reconstruct what they have said in one language, together with others. In other words, we *must betray* our own translational impressions and perceptions for our research and educational activities in order to enrich them.]

['Bad' forms of betraying to me relate to an overreliance on un-reflexive and selectively critical selves as the only source of translation. Therefore, we should betray ourselves by moving beyond over-relying on one's exclusive simplistic acts of translation. Another unsatisfactory form of betraying has to do with *NOT* translating *again and again*, especially together with others. These forms of betraying can have awkward consequences on what and how we write our research, even misleading our conclusions – and thus readers, research participants, students and decision-makers who might read us. Let me take a simple example. Many of us claim to be doing (critical) 'discourse analysis', a highly polysemic term often used as a substitute for mere content analysis, of data that we have collected in different languages, using (often) unchecked translations from these languages into English. By betraying the voices of those whom we examine, resorting to, e.g., a sloppy pronoun use in English (e.g., a generic *you* instead of *a passive voice* in the original language or translating 宣传 'simply' into *propaganda*, while publicity or promotion could work, adding different connotations), without justifying our choices or consulting, e.g., research participants, we might manipulate these voices willy-nilly and thus present our readers with unproblematized 'modified' analyses and interpretations of multilingual realities.

In the book, I am calling for us researchers and educators to accept imperfections in our translation work as a stimulation for listening to others and making sure that the complexities of their voices are heard to do them justice. These imperfections must change through co-engaging with translation. Going back to *Traduttore, traditore*, like translation, the word *betray* also contains a hint at a Latin word for *handing over* and *trader*, which is based on *trans-* (across) and *dare* (to give), *to give across*. Committing to 'good' acts of betrayal in the way we do and use translation in our research on interculturality can help us deal with the communicative, often contradictory and unstable characteristics of the very notion. Accepting and working upon the fact that translation is always transient could make intercultural research and education closer to the complex realities of us meeting each other across multilayered borders. 'Good' acts of betrayal also have to do with the political, which is often ignored or relegated to the position of a 'ghost' in research on intercultural communication education. Translation is always political since it has to do with interpretation, making decisions and positioning. Since interculturality itself is highly political in research and education (Dervin & Simpson, 2021), because it has to do with the way we see and are made to see 'self', 'other', 'relationships' and the 'ideological orders' that we are given to *do* interculturality in, e.g., education, reflecting openly and acting upon translation in research can help us identify and act upon snapshots of politicization indecisions made by ourselves, scholars and educators, including the influences we might be subjected to (e.g., 'Council of Europeanization' of intercultural knowledge), and our own personal agendas in dealing with interculturality. Translation can serve as a central tenet of reflexivity and criticality, alone and/or together with others, so that we might become even more aware of our own political and ideological biases and agendas. As a reminder, translation can serve to abuse others *politically*. I am thinking here of how, e.g., the translation of the title of Darwin's *The Origin of Species by Means of Natural Selection* was 'mistranslated' (or abuslated, abused + translated) by Clémence Royer into *De l'origine des espèces ou des lois du progrès chez les êtres organisés*: On the Origin of Species or the Laws of Progress in Organized Beings (instead of *by Means of Natural Selection*), to send a message against the dominating religious obscurantism of the time in France (see Blanckaert, 1991; Samoyault, 2020).] [*How often do we make such (sub-/conscious) decisions while reporting on our intercultural research? How often do we clarify these choices? How often do we reflect openly on these choices for our readers, linking them up with our own affiliations?*]

[I argue that ignoring translation is both working against interculturality (and contributing to the essentialism that most of us now decry) and hiding/closing our eyes in front of the 'economic-political' decisions that are made in intercultural research and education. The last decade has been filled with increasing calls for social justice, 'democratic culture', the respect of human rights and decoloniality in relation to interculturality (Simpson & Dervin, 2019; R'boul, 2022) and yet, disregarding translation issues in writing about these issues can work against them. Scholars and educators working on interculturality must be the middlemen in communicating around interculturality – instead of its dictators or mere ideologists!]

Translation as the language of interculturality?

[In *Intercultural Competence for Translators* Tomozeiu et al. (2019) argue: "By definition, translators are intercultural mediators". I maintain that "by definition, interculturalists are translators (too)". *As soon as we open our mouths about interculturality, the issue of translation is always relevant, one way or another.* As scholars and educators of interculturality, we cannot be *outside of*, *beyond*, or *above* translation. Translation must be considered as *the* language of interculturality. If the aims of interculturality are to *liaise with* and *care about* others, then for scholars and educators, translation must come first. Intercultural scholars and educators must deterritorialize themselves through language in order to *interculturalize interculturality*, a phrase I have proposed (Dervin, 2021) and worked on with my colleague Andreas Jacobsson (Dervin & Jacobsson, 2022). Interculturalizing interculturality consists in expanding the ways we perceive, conceptualize, discuss and co-construct interculturality *ad infinitum*. No one holds the key to the notion; no one can claim that they can ensnare this fluid and changing notion into a theoretical, conceptual and methodological 'cage'. It also means to move away from 'satisfactory' scholarly and educational positions about the notion, 'digging' *again and again* in its diverse meanings, objectives and (temporary) implementations. The power of language in energizing intercultural research, and education is thus central for communicating around interculturality. I see language through translation as a human face where every nerve, every muscle, every cell is complex and changeable (but also fragile), and our task as interculturalists is to confront these characteristics head-on.]

[I am not telling you here to 'train' to become a translator. As scholars and educators, we are 'non-professional' translators. We don't get judged on, e.g., the literary quality of our translations but on the transparency and capacity to convince that what we do with translation for interculturality is trustworthy *a minima* and that we care 'translationally' about those who read us, listen to us, entrust us with their voices, etc. All I want is for us to think further together about translation for interculturality, to build up more awareness of its centrality. I don't consider myself better than others in including translation in the way I research and teach interculturality. Since 2020, I have incorporated more work on translation in, e.g., intercultural education in the seminars that I give to students in Finland and Mainland China. This is meant to urge them to be more consistent and caring about it, especially when they discuss interculturality in English as a Lingua franca. Let me give you a short example. In the autumn of 2022, some Chinese students dialogued with my Finnish students around conceptions of interculturality in their respective contexts (education, politics and broader society). Since important political decisions related to internal diversity and internationalization had been presented at the National Party Congress of China, the Chinese students were asked to reflect on how these could be explained to their Finnish counterparts in English as a Lingua Franca. A certain number of key phrases and terms had been chosen to (un- and re-)translate between the students first and then with their teachers in class. Here is what one of the students wrote in his diary after these sessions:

> In this course, what impressed me most is that we have talked about how to translate some Chinese policy words related to interculturality into English. The teacher gave ten examples such as "征途", "新发展理念", and showed us the official translations. He thought that the translations were not so good because foreigners don't really know Chinese culture and history. Then we tried to translate these words together again, our group choose "征途". At first, we translated it into 'Always have enthusiasm to struggle', but the teacher suggested that this translation sounded a bit bellicose and that it could be misunderstood by Western audiences, especially since Western media often construct an aggressive image of Mainland

China. He surprised us by advising that we could change 'struggle' to 'Chinese dream' (a phrase that foreigners might understand better). All of us thought that the new translation is not only correct but also beautiful. It looks friendly. So finally, our translation was: 'Aim heartily for the Chinese Dream'. Thanks to this work, I learnt about the power of language and translation as a main method in interculturality.

[The keyword of ethics is increasingly central to communicating around interculturality – as is the case in other fields of the human and social sciences. Languaging and translation are at the core of ethics in education and research on interculturality. The (unacceptable) disappearance of the translator-researcher in dealing with data, leaving us with the impression that the data is 'straightforward' when translated in English, is one such vital issue.]

What do 'interculturalists' have to say about translation?

I hope that I have not given the impression until now that the issue of translation has been ignored in the broad field of interculturality (communication, education, business, nursing, etc.). Let me provide a list of publications (books) in Table 3.1 that could be of interest for exploring this important issue further (2015–2022). I have included some of the classics on the issue (see, e.g., House's work), books concerning difficult aspects of translation and interculturality ('concentration camps') and publications on interpreting – which is a very different process from translation and yet is close to it. Note that some of the books do not claim to work directly on interculturality but on cultures and/or translanguaging. None of these books focus on the very act of communicating around the notion that interests us here but more on interculturality as a phenomenon/encounters.

[Reflexive and critical potpourri]

- After reading this chapter, would you agree that including systematic reflections on the use of language in communicating around interculturality increases our chances of being humbler in dealing with the notion? What does the very word *humility* bring to mind in relation to what is discussed in this book?
- What do you consider to be persistent ideologisms of interculturality in research and education?
- What comes to your mind when you hear the word *translation* in English and other languages? What does it connote? What feelings do you experience and why? How has your engagement with translation in different contexts been?

Table 3.1 Publications focusing on issues of translation for interculturality

Year	Publications
2015	*Translation as Communication across Languages* (House)
2016	*Interpreting in Nazi Concentration Camps* (Wolf)
	Translational Action and Intercultural Communication (Buhrig et al., Eds.)
2017	*Intercultural faultlines: Research models in translation studies: Textual and cognitive aspects* (Olohan, Ed.)
2018	*Mediating emergencies and conflicts: Frontline translating and interpreting* (Federici, Ed.)
2019	*Traduction et interculturalité: Entre identité et altérité* [Translation and interculturality: Between identity and alterity] (Dziub et al., eds.)
	Intercultural aspect in translation and reception of precedent phenomena (Zahorak)
	Intercultural competence for translators (Tomozeiu)
	Hybrid Englishes and the challenges of and for translation: Identity, mobility and language change (Bennett & de Barros)
	Translating across sensory and linguistic borders: Intersemiotic journeys between media (Campbell & Vidal, Eds.)
2020	*Communication across cultures: The linguistics of texts in translation* (Hatim)
2021	*Chinese-English interpreting and intercultural communication* (Hlavac & Xu)
	Intercultural communication in interpreting (Cho)
	Intercultural crisis communication: Translation, interpreting and languages in local crises (Declercq & Federici, Eds.)
	Translating cultures: An introduction for translators, interpreters and mediators (3rd ed.) (Katan & Taibi)
2022	*Translanguaging in translation: Invisible contributions that shape our language and society* (Sato)
	The politics of researching multilingually. Multilingual Matters (Holmes et al.)
	Methodological issues and challenges in researching transculturally (Victoria)

- In the French language, there are at least two phrases where the verb *to translate* (*traduire*) is used beyond a reference to 'moving across' from one language to another: *traduire en justice* (word-for-word translation: *to translate in justice*, i.e., *to prosecute*) and *traduire ses émotions* (word-for-word translation: *to translate one's emotions*, i.e., *to express one's emotions*). Can you think of phrases or idioms in the languages that you know in relation to the idea of translation? What do they tell you about the meanings and connotations of translation in these languages/contexts?
- Here are two quotes by two European intellectuals (a philosopher and a writer) concerning translation. What do these tell us about their conceptions

of the process of translating? Do you find these ideas inspiring, critical, Eurocentric, etc.?

"The process of translating comprises in its essence the whole secret of human understanding of the world and of social communication". (Gadamer, in Schulte & Biguenet, 1992, p. 9)
"Translation is that which transforms everything so that nothing changes". (Grass, 2000, p. 27)

- Now consider this quote from Manguel (2010, p. 21): "The ideal reader is a translator. He or she can pull a text to pieces, remove its skin, cut it to the bone, follow each artery and vein and thence fashion a new living being". What does this tell you about the processes of translating? How do you relate these views with your own work in communicating around interculturality?
- What stereotypes about translation do people around you (colleagues, students, family members) have? How about in other contexts you might have access to? How have they built up these representations?
- A coursebook on translation and interculturality I came across is entitled *Translating Cultures* (Katan & Taibi, 2021). What do you think of this title? What are your views on the idea of *translating cultures*? Is this what we are meant to do as interculturalists? *But what is culture?* What does *translating* this concept mean concretely? Could other aspects of intercultural communication be the focus of translation instead of *culture*? I recommend acquainting yourself with Katan and Taibi's book to get a sense of what they do with this 'old and tired' concept (and its critiques) in the field of translation and interpreting.

[Recommended reading]

Roucek, J. S. (1943). Ideology as a means of social control. *The American Journal of Economics and Sociology, 3*(1), 35–45.

In this classic piece about ideology, Roucek reviews different definitions of the concept. He also speculates about what 'successful' ideologies could be. For instance, he examines the claims of scientific objectivity, realism and universality against ideologism. Although the article was published nearly a century ago, it is a very relevant piece that urges us to unthink and rethink (with) this important concept. I have argued that communicating around interculturality requires placing ideology at the centre of our discussions to allow moving forward and 'balancing otherness with otherness' in the construction of discourses around the notion.

Barthes, R. (2020). *Roland Barthes by Roland Barthes*. Vintage Books.

This important book by the philosopher, literary theorist and semiotician Roland Barthes has inspired me for years. It is, in fact, 'marketed' as an autobiography but it is more than this. In playful manners, Barthes narrates and comments 'snapshots' of his life, discussing his habits, tastes and passions. Language is at the centre of these autobiographical moments, and Barthes urges us to systematically take into account its power and defaults. People working on interculturality cannot but find this book of interest to 'digest' other ways of thinking about and with language reflexively.

Liu, F., Han, D., House, J., & Kadar, D. Z. (2021). The expressions "(M)minzu-zhuyi" and "Nationalism": A contrastive pragmatic analysis. *Journal of Pragmatics, 174*, 168–178.

I wanted to include this fascinating paper from House and Kadar's team here. In cooperation with Chinese colleagues, they have managed to produce stimulating research on the use of different Chinese concepts and expressions, to which I have been very sensitive over the past years. In this paper, they propose a contrastive pragmatic analysis of the expressions *(M)minzu-zhuyi* (民族主义) and *nationalism*, questioning the assumption that nationalism is universally perceived as a negative phenomenon. As such, they show that the Chinese expressions do not correspond directly to the main ideology of nationalism as used in, e.g., the U.S. This important study confirms the importance of reflecting very carefully on the words that we use when analyzing, producing and disseminating knowledge(s) within the broad field of intercultural communication education.

References

Aesop. (2023). *Fables.* https://fablesofaesop.com/tongues.html
Austin, M. (2007). *The American rhythm.* Sunstone Press.
Barthes, R. (1978). *Leçon.* Seuil.
Barthes, R. (1989). *The rustle of language.* University of California Press.
Barthes, R. (2020). *Roland Barthes by Roland Barthes.* Vintage Books.
Bellos, D. (2012). *Is that a fish in your ear? Translation and the meaning of everything.* Penguin.
Bennett, K., & de Barros, R. Q. (Eds.). (2019). *Hybrid Englishes and the challenges of and for translation: Identity, mobility and language change.* Routledge.
Blanckaert, C. (1991). Les bas-fonds de la science française: Clémence Royer, l'origine de l'Homme et le Darwinisme social. *Bulletins et Mémoires de la Société d'Anthropologie de Paris, 1–2,* 115–130.
Buhrig, K., House, J., & Thije, J. T. (Eds.). (2016). *Translational action and intercultural communication.* Routledge.
Byram, M. (1997). *Teaching and assessing intercultural communicative competence.* Multilingual Matters.
Campbell, M., & Vidal, R. (Eds.). (2019). *Translating across sensory and linguistic borders: Intersemiotic journeys between media.* Palgrave Macmillan.
Cho, J. (2021). *Intercultural communication in interpreting.* Routledge.
Cocteau, J. (2013). *The difficulty of being.* Melville House Publishing.
Darvin, R., & Norton, B. (2015). Identity and a model of investment in applied linguistics. *Annual Review of Applied Linguistics, 35,* 36–56.
Declercq, C., & Federici, F. (Eds.). (2021). *Intercultural crisis communication: Translation, interpreting and languages in local crises.* Bloomsbury Academic.
Dervin, F. (2016). *Intercultural education: A theoretical and methodological toolbox.* Palgrave Macmillan.
Dervin, F. (2021, April 19). *Critical and reflexive languaging in the construction of interculturality as an object of research and practice.* Digital Series of Talks on Plurilingualism and Interculturality. University of Copenhagen.
Dervin, F. (2022). *Interculturality in fragments: A reflexive approach.* Springer.
Dervin, F. (2023). *The paradoxes of interculturality.* Routledge.
Dervin, F., & Jacobsson, A. (2021). *Teacher Education for Critical and Reflexive Interculturality.* Palgrave Macmillan.
Dervin, F., & Jacobsson, A. (2022). *Intercultural communication education: Broken realities and rebellious dreams.* Springer.
Dervin, F., & R'boul, H. (2022). *Through the looking-glass of interculturality.* Springer.

Dervin, F., & Simpson, A. (2021). *Interculturality and the political within education*. Routledge.
Dervin, F., Sude, B., Yuan, M., & Chen, N. (2022). *Interculturality between East and West*. Springer.
Dervin, F., & Yuan, M. (2022). Political ideology and atonality in language and intercultural education: A rejoinder to "between professionalism and political engagement in foreign language teaching practice" by Claire Kramsch. *Journal of Applied Linguistics and Professional Practice, 16*(3), 31–45.
Dziub, N., Musinova, T., & Voegele, A. (Eds.). (2019). *Traduction et interculturalité: Entre identité et altérité* [Translation and interculturality: Between identity and alterity]. Peter Lang.
Federici, F. (Ed.). (2018). *Mediating emergencies and conflicts: Frontline translating and interpreting*. Palgrave Macmillan.
Fraser, N. (2022). *Cannibal capitalism*. Verso Books.
Goldsmith, K. (2016). *Against translation*. Jean Boite.
Gordin, M. D. (2015). *Scientific Babel*. Chicago university Press.
Grass, G. (2000). *Dog years*. Vintage.
Hatim, B. (2020). *Communication across cultures: The linguistics of texts in translation*. University of Exeter Press.
Hlavac, J., & Xu, Z. (2021). *Chinese-English interpreting and intercultural communication*. Routledge.
Ho, W. Y. (2022). "Coming here you should speak Chinese": The multimodal construction of interculturality in YouTube videos. *Language and Intercultural Communication, 22*(6), 662–680.
Hofstede, G., Hofstede, G. J. & Minkov, M. (2010). *Cultures and Organizations: Software of the Mind*. McGraw Hill.
Holliday, A. (2010). *Intercultural communication and ideology*. Sage.
Holmes, P., Dooly, M., & O'Regan, J. (Eds.). (2018). *Intercultural dialogue: Questions of research, theory, and practice*. Routledge.
Holmes, P., Reynolds, J., & Ganassin, S. (Eds.). (2022). *The politics of researching multilingually*. Multilingual Matters.
House, J. (2015). *Translation as communication across languages*. Routledge.
House, J., Kadar, D. Z., Liu, F., & Han, D. (2022). The problem of translating Chinese policy-related expressions: A case study of *wenming* ("civilised"). *Text & Talk*, OnlineFirst. https://doi.org/10.1515/text-2021-0142
Katan, D., & Taibi, M. (2021). *Translating cultures: An introduction for translators, interpreters and mediators*. Routledge.
Kim, Y. K. (2007). Ideology, identity, and intercultural communication: An analysis of differing academic conceptions of cultural identity. *Journal of Intercultural Communication Research, 36*(3), 237–253.
LaCapra, D. (1988). Culture and ideology: From Geertz to Marx. *Poetics Today, 9*, 377–394.
Liu, F., Han, D., House, J., & Kadar, D. Z. (2021). The expressions "(M)minzu-zhuyi" and "Nationalism": A contrastive pragmatic analysis. *Journal of Pragmatics, 174*, 168–178.
Manguel, A. (2010). *A reader on reading*. Yale University Press.
Murdoch, I. (2014). *Connected: Critical essays*. The University of Tennessee Press.
NBC News. (2023). Gwen Stefani's response to cultural appropriation charges. *NBC News*. www.nbcnews.com/news/asian-america/gwen-stefani-says-japanese-response-cultural-appropriation-charges-rcna65203

Oldfield, J. (2022). Racing neoliberalism and remote Indigenous education in the Northern Territory of Australia: a critical analysis of contemporary Indigenous education language policy and practice, Language and Intercultural Communication 22(6), 694–708, DOI: 10.1080/14708477.2022.2046018

Olohan, M. (Ed.). (2017). *Intercultural faultlines: Research models in translation studies: Textual and cognitive aspects*. Routledge.

Orwell, G. (2001). *Orwell and politics*. Penguin.

Phipps, A. (2014). "They are bombing now": "Intercultural dialogue" in times of conflict. *Language and Intercultural Communication, 14*(1), 108–124.

Piller, I. (2011). *Intercultural communication: A critical introduction*. Edinburgh University Press.

Pullum, G. K. (1991). *The Great Eskimo vocabulary hoax and other irreverent essays on the study of language*. University of Chicago Press.

R'boul, H. (2022). Epistemological plurality in intercultural communication knowledge. *Journal of Multicultural Discourses, 17*, 173–188. https://doi.org/10.1080/17447143.2022.2069784

Roucek, J. S. (1943). Ideology as a means of social control. *The American Journal of Economics and Sociology, 3*(1), 35–45.

Roucek, J. S. (1944). A history of the concept of ideology. *Journal of the History of Ideas, 5*(4), 479–488.

Rowell, J. (1995). The politics of cultural appropriation. *Journal of Value Inquiry, 29*, 137–142.

Samoyault, T. (2020). *Traduction et violence*. Seuil.

Sato, E. (2022). *Translanguaging in translation: Invisible contributions that shape our language and society*. Multilingual Matters.

Schulte, R., & Biguenet, J. (Eds.). (1992). *Theories of translation: An anthology of essays from Dryden to Derrida*. The University of Chicago.

Simpson, A., & Dervin, F. (2019). Global and intercultural competences for whom? By whom? For what purpose? An example from the Asia society and the OECD. *Compare: A Journal of Comparative and International Education, 49*(4), 672–677.

Skutnabb-Kangas, T., & Phillipson, R. (Eds.). (1995). *Linguistic human rights: Overcoming linguistic discrimination*. New York: Mouton de Gruyter.

Thompson, G., & Dooley, K. (2019). Ensuring translation fidelity in multilingual research. In J. McKinley & H. Rose (Eds.), *The Routledge handbook of research methods in applied linguistics* (pp. 63–75). Routledge.

Tomozeiu, D., Koskinen, K., & D'Arcangelo, A. (Eds.). (2019). *Intercultural competence for translators*. Routledge.

Verkuyten, M., Yogeeswaran, K., Mepham, K., & Sprong, S. (2020). Interculturalism: A new diversity ideology with interrelated components of dialogue, unity, and identity flexibility. *European Journal of Social Psychology, 50*(3), 505–519.

Victoria, M. (2022). *Methodological issues and challenges in researching transculturally*. Cambridge Scholars Publishing.

Wisman, J. D. (2023). Why ideology exists. *Journal of Economic Issues, 57*(1), 200–217.

Wittgenstein, L. (1975). *On Certainty*. Wiley.

Wolf, M. (2016). *Interpreting in Nazi concentration camps*. Bloomsbury.

Zahorak, A. (2019). *Intercultural aspect in translation and reception of precedent phenomena*. Peter Lang.

Zembylas, M. (2023). The affective ideology of the OECD global competence framework: Implications for intercultural communication. *Pedagogy, Culture & Society, 31*(2), 305–323.

4 Nurturing and galvanizing

[Vocalizing]

1. Based on your reading of the previous chapters, what changes might you want to implement in your communicating around interculturality in your own educational contexts and with colleagues from other parts of the world?
2. In this chapter, I address some themes that have been neglected in research and education: the right to un/dream, insecurities, contradictions-inconsistencies, hesitations and subjectivities (amongst others). Review each of these issues for yourself before reading the chapter. What might they refer to? How important are they to you?
3. How often do you listen carefully to the 'un-heard' of interculturality, e.g., people in powerless positions whose voices we tend to mediate and which tend to be merely 'reproduced', 'interpreted' and 'mentioned in passing'? For example, how many times has one of your students or someone on the streets pushed you to think outside your own comfort zone about interculturality?

Prologue

I

What the previous chapters have hinted at is that language for communicating around interculturality can be an *impasse,* although it might appear as a *passe-partout.* Communicating around a complex notion that has been with us for several decades in English and some languages (Chinese and Finnish, for example, have an equivalent word for *interculturality* but an unstable construct which many people easily substitute with other words) could be deemed challenging not just because it is hard to communicate around it. As we have seen in previous chapters, the inflation of voices, silences, dominating ideologies and disregard for languaging but also because of a lack of arenas and opportunities for communication can be detrimental to meaningful, long-term engagement around the notion.

DOI: 10.4324/9781003451938-4

II

Although dialogue seems to be happening through thousands of publications and (online) events each year, it is clear that these dialogues are scattered, linguistically, institutionally and socially divided and divisive, unequal and potentially performative rather than engaging. The complex worlds of interculturality in research and education are composed of different institutional, ideological, geopolitical and guru-centric 'tribes' (on academic tribes, see Becher, 2001), which rarely interact directly, increasingly through citations and referencing mostly to negate each other's contribution. Often, the other tribe's voice is simply invalidated, censored and boycotted, leaving space for promoting one's own people.

III

In the era of decolonizing we are witnessing (R'boul, 2022; Danping, 2022), interculturality is slowly being deconstructed to provide some space for what is often referred to today as the Global South. *Who talks and urges for decoloniality and who acts for it* is another question. Since academia tends to be based on privilege and authority, it is hard for people not located in powerful centres (and even with specific nationalities and 'first' languages) to be heard. Fame and influence in relation to interculturality in research and education still seems to revolve around powerful ('Western') affiliations and production in the English language (amongst others) (on international knowledge acquisition, production, transfer, circulation, networks, and the geopolitics of science, see Shen et al., 2022).

I also have the impression that there could be some form of resistance to 'alternative' knowledge or 'disruptive' ways of doing research on interculturality, especially against accepted norms and ideologies. Recently I noticed with a colleague of mine from the Global South that several countries in North Africa were organizing conferences on interculturality for which the main keynote speakers were from the U.K. and the U.S. (white, senior, retired professors). *Privileged scholars are still talking about the notion, even in former colonial contexts.* As a white 'privileged' scholar myself, I now refuse to speak in the Global South unless I am given a secondary position or asked to engage with colleagues from the Global South – rather than merely 'speaking', which often means speaking *over* and *for* others in the case of a keynote speech.

IV

Learning to communicate around interculturality cannot be a specific act/process. To teach others how to communicate in specific ways (how and what to (not) say) is to force them into ideological silos. This is not what I endeavor to do in this chapter, although I feel that I could be on the verge of pushing through certain (counter-)ideologies willy-nilly. I use two keywords for us to think further about takeaways concerning communication around interculturality: *nurture* and *galvanize*. Nurture is from Latin and has to do with upbringing, but also (and more importantly) nourishing (food) and suckling. I take the word as urging us to reflect further on what, who, how and why we should/ could communicate around interculturality in research and education beyond mere indoctrination, silencing and reproducing dominating ideologies. The verb *to galvanize* started to be used in English in the 19th century based on a French word that had to do with stimulating by galvanic electricity. To galvanize is about excitation and stimulation. I believe that nurturing and galvanizing are two sides of the same coin when reflecting further on communication.

Some 'remices'

This subsection shares some of my reflections (called 'remices' – 'remarks-advice') based on my reviews of research articles during the past three years. I have reformulated these reviews in general terms in what follows. I need to remind the reader that I am treading on eggs here since each of these 'remices' probably contains ideological elements that I would not want to impose on anyone. I am sharing them since they can represent proposals for dealing with some of the issues concerning communication highlighted in previous chapters. Please feel free to be as critical as you wish in front of my remarks-advice.

[Words are never innocent, as was discussed many times before in the book. Writing in a 'big' language like English in academia, I can never take things for granted; even the 'smallest' and 'most obvious' word – but is anything ever obvious? The use of words such as (randomly) 'interculturalism', 'nationalities', 'ethnic', 'inter-ethnic communication', 'minority', 'spirit', can be very problematic if they are not spelt out. Nationalities in English, for example, might mean very different things in different parts of the world and not merely refer to someone's passport (as is the tendency in Northern Europe). Different economic-political (research and educational) contexts might position these terms in specific ways. We should not take their meanings and connotations for granted.]

[Reviewing papers written by scholars from outside my own 'corner' of the world, I struggle at times to make sense of some of the concepts, notions and ideologemes that they use – as much as they probably find it hard to position mine! Here are examples of such elements: 'communication attitude', 'social culture', 'national unity' and 'cultural intellectual humility'. Although we might get an idea of what these refer to as we read them (some appearing to be word-to-word translations), we need to explain them *a minima* to ensure further communication, even within the framework of an article or a book.

Recently I was discussing a paper with a Chinese colleague who had used the idea of "poor quality schools" to refer to some schools in the Chinese context. She seemed to take it for granted that international audiences would easily understand what this phrase referred to concretely. However, the criteria for such schools in China, Botswana and Finland would differ immensely.]

[Some of the words we use might also have been borrowed from other ideological contexts, which requires problematizing their use. It is fine obviously to use, e.g., a 'European' concept such as *intercultural citizenship* masquerading as a 'global' construct, if we provide some answers to these questions concerning our own research: 1. Are these concepts understandable and meaningful in my context (especially by those we 'study' and/or train)? 2. How can they be renegotiated *glocally* so that they don't clash 'too much' with other ideologies? 3. Can their meanings be modified and combined with other meanings? 4. How compatible are they with local political discourses? (By this, I mean: how do they fit into the 'narratives' that local educational institutions spread?), etc.]

[The question of giving access to different kinds of knowledge to ensure 'fairer' communication around interculturality is essential. However, the following questions need to be addressed: 1. What do we do with this multifaceted knowledge? 2. How can we make it enter into meaningful dialogues with other kinds of knowledge that can lead to *new forms of knowledge*? 3. How do we empower people who are not part of more global discussions around interculturality to voice their disagreements and add to the discussions?]

[References would need to move beyond the 'core' 'Western' literature, meaning from scholars located outside the dominating centre of knowledge production in English. I have read so many articles about Chinese Minzu 'minority' education, for example, that contain far too many 'Western' references to be credible *ideologically*. The Minzu context is very specific and deserves to be dealt with, looking into Chinese scholarship *too*. For example, using Western canons such as Bernstein or Bourdieu does not really make much sense and do justice to these complexities. The systematic and meaningful inclusion of references off-the-centre matters for ALL aspects of our research (from theory to analysis). It is hard work since we need to identify and discover relevant literature, often in languages other than English, and yet this is needed more than ever.]

[Can an American scholar based at a prestigious U.S. institution working on intercultural teacher education *in China* (for Minzu students) really contribute to renewing 'Chinese training' while using knowledge produced by their own team and other scholars *in the U.S.*? Reading through their publications, one clearly sees a preference for U.S.-based ideologies of diversity in education and culturally-responsive teaching, 'attacking' China for not preparing her teachers by, e.g., making use of key concepts related to, e.g., multicultural education or critical race theory. I am left to wonder what multicultural education we are talking about here and who could choose 'key concepts' from it that would be applicable to the Chinese context. As we know, multicultural education (although the term is polysemic, too) was developed in specific economic-political contexts, especially in the U.S. and U.K., so can we assume that it should be adopted (blindly) and accepted in other contexts? By looking into Chinese teacher education through these 'lenses', some form of knowledge or economic-political ideology is superimposed in a different context (dare I say that this is a form of 'neo-imperialism'?). Finally, does using, e.g., frameworks developed for studying migrant children in the U.S. make sense to make proposals for Chinese (intercultural) teacher education for Minzu contexts? Is justifying an 'attack' against Minzu education by quoting, e.g., American scholar James Banks (who has never studied Minzu education in Chinese on the spot) a good idea?]

[I remember reading a paper written by a scholar from the U.K. about Chinese Minzu education in which he used a reference from an American scholar published 20 years earlier to justify current problems about this form of education.]

[The stereotyping of the dichotomy of intercultural/multicultural education needs complexifying. Dividing them into North American and European does not reveal the *complex* realities of these fields in the 'West' and elsewhere. The dichotomy of *multicultural* and *intercultural* is still used today in research politics to defend one's views and superiority (Joppke, 2018). While we discuss these, fighting with ideologies and economic-political agendas, the (real) world is in trouble.]

[In many research articles using mostly 'Western-centric' ideologies, I often feel some form of discursive violence – as if they were saying: I cannot hear you; I am not listening to you; maybe I don't even know that you exist! I have often mistreated the other in the same way in my work.]

[In fact, there is no West. There is no such thing as the 'West'. The phrase 'Western-centric', which I abuse myself, does not make much sense. In the so-called 'West', whose borders are difficult to define, not everybody has the same influence on others, not everybody is allowed to speak, not everybody has access to privileges. The 'West' could, in fact, be imaginary. And yet, we know that some of us in the 'West' dominate and overly influence the ways others think, do research and educate interculturally.]

[Another issue concerns being trained to identify the potential economic-political and ideological manipulations hidden behind *knowledge* (for example, when it emerges from the OECD and/or the Council of Europe). The central issue is (again) language: what are the meanings and connotations of concepts/notions, ideas, arguments, etc.? How do we re-enunciate from a translingual/multilingual perspective while being aware of politics-ideologies?]

[Who the researcher is in terms of nationality, ethnicity, race, gender, social class, etc. always matters in research, and yet these are very rarely spelt out. For example, a white male middle-aged professor interviewing a group of local teachers in English in, e.g., Kazakhstan, will not have the same influence on their research participants as, e.g., a local male Ph.D. student. What might be said might differ immensely. This is why, for instance, the language skills of the scholar must be introduced in our work (see Victoria, 2022).]

[Any form of intercultural training always relies on 'indoctrination' one way or another. What I mean is: the way we scholars and educators teach (about) interculturality is always *political – we pass on ideologies, beliefs and certainties for a notion that should not be considered under such lenses.* This always relates to the way we see 'self', 'other', 'society', 'community', etc. and the way we talk about them (see the political project of Democratic culture) (Barrett & Golubeva, 2022). These issues are not 'objective' *things* but constructions based on socio-economic-political views. When, e.g., as a visiting professor, one teaches about interculturality in China willy-nilly, one 'imports' these views, often without realizing (maybe). For example, we might use the concept of 'race' or 'tolerance' without realizing that they are not universally understood. All these choices cannot but be based on the way (g/local) political beliefs, memberships (or not) have made us think about interculturality in certain ways – not just so-called scientific knowledge. These need to be put forward transparently, reflected upon in teaching and negotiated with students and colleagues. We have the duty to remind our readers and trainees that we are aware of this central problem.]

[What research participants say during interviews is not 'litany'. We need to analyze what they say to show, e.g., their potential contradictions and how much we also seem to influence them in the way they describe their realities.]

[A lot of our research participants' comments may contain stereotypes about different kinds of people. We need to deconstruct them instead of taking them at face value – as if they represented some kind of 'truth'.]

[A lot of what we write and say about interculturality might be stereotypical. We need to recognize moments of stereotyping in us and listen more carefully to what, e.g., research participants are saying. Our questions might push them to go in directions that they might not want to explore or to say things that they might not want to say. Working with a group of 'local' students recently who were about to interview international students from the same institution, we negotiated together the way they might want to formulate their questions. At first, the students wished to ask them about the kinds of problems they were facing at the university (mostly focusing on problems). We agreed that an indirect question such as 'how do you imagine the experience of local students to be at this university?' would be a better way of trying to find out about their own experiences, since we assumed that they would draw potential comparisons by themselves.]

[Contextualising lesser-known contexts of interculturality is essential when communicating around it. Things that are obvious to us may not be to outsiders. Going back to Minzu, a lot of geo-political, ideological contextualization is constantly necessary to make the notion as transparent as possible to others. Many discourses around the notion in Chinese are 'untranslatable' in English and deserve to be treated carefully.]

[Not mentioning in what language(s) our data were collected and not problematizing how they were translated is both a breach of ethics and a central issue of research validity (Holmes et al., 2022). If the data were collected in, e.g., Tagalog, what problems did the authors have in translating them into English? We might consider inserting the originals so that the reader can get a real sense of what these participants were saying. Too many studies ignore this vital aspect of research on interculturality. Language is not just a guest but a main actor.]

[Examining interculturality in education in another country is itself a political act, which cannot but be guided by ideological clashes. Authors must be transparent about their motivations: *why did they really study a given context? What is their involvement with politics of interculturality in education in the 'host country' and elsewhere? Is the paper a scientific and/or a political project?* Observing and examining another context will often lead to comparisons, which might lead to judgements. This is why it is important to 'watch' our words so that we don't appear to be 'evaluating' in ways that are unfair and unfounded 'scientifically' (if this is ever possible).]

Listening to the 'half' un-heard

In my recent publications, I have often given the floor directly to students with whom I have engaged (Dervin & Tan, 2022; Dervin & Chen, 2023). My main motivation is to give back to them and to acknowledge their immense inspirational power in my work. I have noticed, however, that some of my colleagues and readers are somewhat put off by the inclusion of their voices, arguing that they are 'just' students. In research on interculturality, we spend a lot of time communicating with students, either to obtain data from them for our 'precious' publications or to 'teach' them, keeping the hierarchy of professors-students in order. Students are 'heard' somehow in our work, but their voices are always 'governed' by our ordering (we classify their voices), analyzing (we 'interpret' what they say) and ideologizing (we draw conclusions and often judge how 'interculturally competent' they are). Often, we scholars and teachers treat ourselves as *superior* to them. The older I get, the more I get frustrated by such attitudes because I do not believe that we are any 'better' than students since, like them, we need to struggle and perform balancing acts with others interculturally on a permanent basis. Our views on what interculturality is and what it entails might have been published in 'important' journals or books, spoken at 'international' events and cited by people from around the world, and yet, as social beings, we cannot claim to be 'superhumans of interculturality' who can judge if others are doing it right. As has become clear throughout this book, languaging around interculturality and 'doing' it is far too complex to be reduced to 'successful' or 'unsuccessful'.

In what follows, I am including the voices of the 'half' un-heard, through which students speak for themselves and (indirectly) about some of the issues that we have discussed hitherto. The texts were originally in English, and they derive from diaries written during a course that I gave on interculturality in 2022. For a six-month period, some of my students discussed the contents and ways of communicating in video-recordings of lectures by international colleagues. These should be considered *paratexts* (Genette, 1979), texts that relate, comment and add to a main text – in this case, the context of a series of lectures on lectures. They provide entry into my 'virtual' lecture hall, showing how some of my students take onboard some of the discussions from previous chapters – or how we nurture and galvanize each other. This also represents an opportunity to observe the different voices that enter the lecture hall, how my *voices* might influence the students (by forcing them to rethink a word in either/or ways), how they seem to accept and/or question them, etc. What the students wrote in their diaries is left verbatim below. I recommend paying attention to the words that they use in English as an indication of their own complex ideological worlds.

["Reflection and reminiscence are interesting, and there is a blurred line between them. Reflection is about taking an objective and critical approach to oneself and keeping the good points and reducing the bad points in the future. Reminiscence is about treating oneself with an inclusive attitude, embellishing past experiences so that the unpleasant or dishonorable things are modified or forgotten. Everyone is able to see the world differently due to their own experiences. I can never see the world as you see it and as you see me, and even though the two may be similar, we can never know the degree of similarity. Reflection is like piecing together the world, or piecing together the real (like a jigsaw). Although each scholar has a different definition of the real and the possibility of its existence, we all have an experience of it" (Student 1).]

["Please accept experience discomfort and conflict instead of judging straight away. In Chinese, we say, "忠言逆耳利于行", which means *sincere reproofs* or *though unpleasant to ears, benefits conducts*. For me, maybe there is another way for people to listen to and take advice.

Interculturality exists in the same country. For example, the climate in my hometown Hulunbeir in Northern China has snow in May, but the climate in Nanjing is warm in May. Interculturality also exists in the same area or even at home. I don't have completely the same hobbies as my friends, but it will not affect our relationships, because we always share interesting things. So we have interculturality in our friendship" (Student 2).]

["In class discussions, I also raised the question: "Why do we use intercultural instead of cross-cultural"? In my previous studies, I have always used the latter, and I think there are differences between these. However, after this lecture, I suddenly found that there was no difference between them, just different linguistic usage habits. You can use any word to express the concept of 'interculturality', including *intercultural, multicultural, transcultural*, etc. But you only need to know what you are talking about and their definition for yourself and others. Another difference is that we have different interpretations. Many scholars have clearly defined it, but I think we should not treat it so narrowly. It is broad and infinite" (Student 3).]

["When we say the same word in two separate languages, we might experience it differently. This is the case for a word like friendship in Chinese and English. First of all, when we talk about "Youshan" 友善 in Chinese, there is the picture of *holding hands*. Moreover, we think not only of the relationship between friends hand by hand, but also of the friendship between countries. They are all higher levels. But when speaking English, we often think of words like *friends, pals*, etc." (Student 4).]

["For example, the translation of YOUSHAN into 'friendship' is not very accurate. YOUSHAN in Chinese is more a way of communicating with people, advocating citizens to participate in social life in a positive and harmonious way" (Student 5).]

["'友善' in China mainly refers to a kind of mutual goodwill between people who want each other to be good, and a kind of mutual friendly feelings generated on this basis. As a core value, friendliness refers to mutual respect, mutual understanding, mutual tolerance, mutual care and mutual help among citizens to form a harmonious social situation in which all citizens are equal, friendly and harmonious. In English translation, "友善" is 'friendship', which mainly refers to the friendly relationship between friends. This word will appear deviation in the understanding of Chinese and English, reflecting the different ways of thinking caused by different cultures" (Student 6).]

["Another example is *bicycle*. People in our grandparents' generation used to call it "yangche". "Yang" means *western* and *overseas*. Since the bicycle was 'imported' by the West into China, it bore a trace of its foreign 'import'. But now we seldom hear this word because bicycles are so common in our daily lives. It can be seen everywhere in the streets and has become a necessity to Chinese" (Student 7).]

["This week, Professor Dervin shared a thought-provoking point with us. He said the word *tolerance* can have two meanings. The first meaning is that you tolerate others, but still believe you are right. It means that you may be able to tolerate their words and behavior, but you never put yourself in their shoes and think about their culture and believe you are magnanimous enough to tolerate others' seemingly 'incorrect' words and behaviors. The second meaning is that you really take into account the cultural background of others, and then you change your habitual thinking patterns, and finally think that what others say or do is also reasonable and right. I think the first kind of tolerance is a kind of hypocrisy. Without really understanding other people's cultures and recognizing them, and just wanting to show their own good character, they take a higher position to 'forgive' other people's behavior that is 'wrong' in their view. Therefore, what we need to do is not to pretend to 'tolerate' others when they do something you don't approve of,

Nurturing and galvanizing 75

but to really put ourselves in the shoes of others' cultures and respect them" (Student 8).]

["Prof. Dervin also shared with us a difference between Finland and China. He tells us that the word 'ideology' may be negative in the 'West'. However, the meaning of the word is neutral in China. This made me realize that sometimes conflicts or even clashes between two countries can be caused by language. Also, sometimes such semantic differences may cause quarrels between the two peoples. Thus, I think language cannot be separated from context and culture, and it is easy to misunderstand when it is taken out of context" (Student 9).]

["When I say words in Chinese and English, I have a different feeling. Some words are hard to explain specifically in Chinese, not to mention in English. Like "和" (Harmony), it's about people getting along with others, it is an important concept in Chinese philosophy. But what is the real meaning of it? No one can just interpret it in a few words" (Student 10).]

["In this lesson, Fred organized us to answer some questions in the form of drawings on paper. The questions were about the differences and similarities between China and the 'West'. I was a little shocked that we were writing about the differences very smoothly, but met some jams when writing about the similarities. When someone thinks of a similarity, there is another voice in our heads, someone who asks: *Are they really like that?* Because it feels like Westerners are individualistic, they seem to have more diversity. Moreover, some very obvious similarities are not too good to write about since they don't appear to be exciting. So, through the task it struck me that we think too much about the differences and ignore some of the commonalities in interculturalism. That is worthy of our attention" (Student 11).]

Nurturing and galvanizing as forms of discovering ourselves anew

[We must discover ourselves anew in each act of communication concerning interculturality as an object of research and education. We must accept clashes within self and between self and others in the process – clashes that we can address at moment x, moment y or never. A small change in our ways of speaking and listening is a victory for interculturality.]

[Communication around interculturality in research and education should not shy away from the personal, individual experiences, our own biases and impressions. Closing the door to what has happened to us as persons *interculturally* when (re-)negotiating discourses of interculturality removes important aspects of what we think, ideologize and problematize. This means revising the fallacy of objectivity seriously.]

[An example of mis-/non-communication amongst the 'converted': An email list where everyone follows a guru's 'orders' to promote democracy and human rights with interculturality; a member sends a message concerning a specific country, condemning their behaviours towards a given people. *No response. No engagement.* No preached 'savoir s'engager'. Silence. Denounce the proselytization of interculturality! Say what it is: indoctrination shying away from real actions.]

[Who do we (not) dare to communicate with? Who are we made to communicate with? Who are we not entitled to communicate with? Who influences the way we communicate around interculturality? Can we free ourselves from some of these *shackles*, even temporarily?]

[Pastiching Cioran (1983, p. 103), one could say that "to communicate is to run after insecurity". Too many discourses of interculturality are too self-assured.]

[We should relearn how to communicate beyond flattering, privileging, boasting and fetishizing concepts, people and ideas, but also beyond negating, silencing, destroying and censoring. In other words: abandoning oneself, one's thinking and speaking habits and reflexes, references, certitudes and reticence, andaccepting one's contradictions and hesitations, looking for contradictions, inconsistencies and hesitations in self and other. Communicating around interculturality requires sharing inner and dialogical discussions with others.]

[Do we need to *understand* everything to be able to communicate? Let's leave space for non-understanding, silence, and confusion. These could lead to further engagement.]

[Communicating around interculturality should trigger both anxiety of the unknown and the desire to explore it. *Anxiety* is usually not perceived as an attractive element in research and education, and yet I do believe that it can and must urge us to listen, to unthink-rethink carefully, to ask questions and to be patient. At the same time, we need to push each other outside our own comfort zones. Interculturality is too intricate and serious to allow any of us scholars and/or educators to be self-sufficient, too certain or 'superior' to it. *Honesty and modesty first.*]

[There is a need for amnesia (e.g., by consciously losing our ideological 'memories') in relation to the way we problematize interculturality so that we can open up to others. At the same time, we must also allow ourselves to dream openly, detangling our/others' beliefs, ideologies, hopes and certainties. *What is it that we would want from intercultural encounters? How would we want to modify the way we have been made to think and thus engage with others around this polysemic notion?*]

[Communicate with what disturbs us, not with what confirms our beliefs and illusions. For example, read books and articles from those who are (said to be) 'controversial', 'culturalist' or 'old-fashioned'. Throughout my career, the most inspiring moments have been those when I have engaged with ideas I thought were not worth exploring. The 'shaking' that they trigger in us is the key to constant renewal.]

[Bearing in mind the inherent contradictions and instabilities of communication, with Orwell (in Hanley, 2020, p. 106) we discover ourselves anew unthinking/rethinking: "To know and not to know, to be conscious of complete truthfulness while telling carefully constructed lies, to hold simultaneously two opinions which cancelled out, knowing them to be contradictory and believing in both of them, to use logic against logic, to repudiate morality while laying claim to it, (. . .) to forget whatever it was necessary to forget, then to draw it back into memory again at the moment when it was needed, and then promptly to forget it again: and above all, to apply the same process to the process itself".]

[We must broaden our experiences of communicating with each other around interculturality rather than merely satisfy our expectations.]

[Our comfort with communication around interculturality might have a lot to do with our temperament. Observing, respecting and learning to deal with different types of people orally and/or in writing can guide us towards un-re-learning interculturality as an object of research and education.]

[In *Ways of Seeing*, Berger (2008, p. 75) asserts: "The relation between what we see and what we know is never settled. Each evening we see the sun set. We know that the earth is turning away from it. Yet the knowledge, the explanation, never quite fits the sight". Re-discovering the triad of knowledge-explanation-sight as far as communicating around interculturality should be a priority.]

[In communicating with others about interculturality, I/you/we need to address our own criticality by being critical of it. Identifying, observing and problematizing problems in others' ways of conceptualizing interculturality also deserve identifying, observing and problematizing problems in the ways we identify, observe and problematize these problems. *The circle of criticality*. Be aware of self indoctrination, brainwashing, over-confidence . . .]

Exploring

[Communicating around interculturality is not about deciding who is right or wrong (everybody is right and wrong in co-constructing discourses around this 'treacherous' notion). We help each other expand our views by looking into the mirror and telling each other – from the side – what we could expect of each other. Revising our thoughts again and again is central to communicating around the notion. Camus (2013, p. 211) criticizes what he calls the 'most serious problem of his time': *conformism* – of which interculturality should be intolerant.]

[Ideas should not possess us. They are always incomplete, never fully formed. Ideas should lead us to the other, to reshape them *ad infinitum*. A complete idea is an ideology. It can easily turn into an order, an agenda or a windscreen. A complete idea about interculturality kills communication.]

[What people tell us about their take on interculturality might not always correspond to their inner thoughts or to the way they have experienced interculturality. Considering the large amount of (silenced) voices that we all face in the process, we might be reciting and recycling discourses without believing in them and without necessarily understanding what they mean, believing that these are the words that we need to use in communication with others. Behind our 'official masks', one might find more complex engagement with the notion. This is why 'honest' and meaningful dialogue – accepting, for instance, that there are more layers of complexity to what we say – can help us develop and renegotiate our thoughts with others.]

[The French tenor Benjamin Berheim (2022) explains: "Gary Magby (Berheim's first teacher) had the wisdom, rather than teaching me how to sing a note, to teach me how to let my body sing it in peace and let my voice not be hindered by parasitic thoughts. (. . .) He told me that you have to be in agreement with your path [voiE in French] to understand your voice [voiX in French]. And this is something that came up very, very often in his class; he told me that these two [with a play upon words in French on the homonym voice] do not always want to go in the same direction".[1] *Find your own path by letting your entire body, your every pore, sing, not merely parroting others' voices when it comes to communicating around interculturality.*]

["Every separation represents a bond", reminds Weil (in Von der Ruhr, 2006, p. 121). Walls constructed between us geo-economic-politically today (and in the past; current walls 'communicate' with the past) which affect research and education, must be considered through the process of *linking*. Although we try hard to be rational and objective in research and education, some of the 'baddies' that we have constructed today get rejected epistemologically, creatively and intellectually because of the walls we are setting up. Interculturality is never a rosy phenomenon, and walls have always existed. However, when communicating around it, we should remember to lift some of these walls to include the silenced, the unheard and the powerless.]

[In Chinese 完美不必无缺 (which can translate as *perfection with flaws*) refers to repairing a defect in a work of art – e.g., leaving beautified traces of repair with gold or emphasizing a defect – turning it into something aesthetically unique and appealing (see Kaniskan, 2018 about Japanese Kintsugi – 'the beauty of wound scars'). Accepting imperfection in what is considered beautiful should be part and parcel of how and why we communicate with each other around interculturality. Things can never be perfect; things must change. In some of his lectures about processes of composing and conducting, Pierre Boulez (1986) problematizes the importance of incompleteness in these creative moments. Incompleteness as a focus of conversation around the notion of interculturality appears to be stimulating. Since interculturality never stops (no one could claim to be ready for it), communicating around it should place incompleteness at its core to observe, problematize and question it.]

[Slowing down the pace of our 'all-communication' era (publish or perish, apply for 'new' projects, give lectures around the world) could allow deeper and more fruitful contributions to the world of interculturality that appears to be collapsing in front of our eyes today.]

[Caring about 'words']

[Communicating around interculturality requires finding new ways and forms of communication. Besides content, the ways we formulate and present things (e.g., in the way they are written) should reflect the diversities that we are urged to promote in research and education. Power relations will not be questioned if we still follow – are forced to follow – the 'standards' imposed on us by a 'Western-centric', (suspiciously) 'rational' and 'objectivizing' system of thought. Ideological 'redecoration' does not suffice if the foundations remain.]

[Listening is central in the processes described here. For the composer Lachenmann (1996, pp. 116–118, translation by Clarkson, 2005): "The capacity to discover in oneself new antennae, new sensors, new sensibilities; to discover one's own alterability and use it to resist the unfreedom which it uncovers. Listening means discovering oneself anew; it means changing oneself". When communicating around interculturality, the audience and producers of words must learn new ways of listening to each other.]

[A good listener is someone who is ready to change at any time by exploring others' ways of speaking and listening, as well as others' words. If there is one 'competence' for interculturality, this one is central.]

[A good communicator around interculturality should be a good listener first and foremost, someone who can pause, be silent and work with and against languaging. Generosity about time, space and voices matters, too, as it is the key to change.]

[I have hinted at the impression that we often 'float past each other' in communicating around interculturality, either by claiming ideological superiority (often disguised under such words as theory) or by using words we take for granted that would require renegotiating. In order to get across to each other, there is a need to limit monologues or dialogues that pretend to be two-way. This is why it is always interesting to ask *why questions* (why this word? Why this scholar? Why this approach?) which urge all of us to stop, think and potentially revise with others. For example, every time I criticize/disregard a concept and/or an argument, I must pause, listen, observe and ask myself *why*? (*why am I attracted to this concept, this ideology? Why do I find them un-/exceptional? How do I limit their magnetism to continue exploring?*). Going back to self in mirroring processes is also central in communicating with others.]

[To speak is to classify; to speak is (often) about imposing our ideas, thoughts and ways of seeing the world. This is why it is important to relearn the words that we use to describe interculturality, together with others, to break away from the 'usual' phrasing and to open up to other ways. One way of doing this might consist in reproducing the idea of *jinhuidui* (literally 'a pile of beautiful things from ash') from Chinese art, which consists in combining, e.g., discarded sketches, ragged brushes, notes, bronzeware (which could be considered as 'ruined fragments') onto paper in a jumble of layers. Although such compositions might appear random, they might look 'differently' sophisticated in their own rearranged way. In a similar manner, we need to look for inspiration in all kinds of situations in life (the arts, a chance encounter, a poem . . .), mixing and reshaping these elements together to recreate other takes about interculturality with others. The metaphor of the sponge might be a good one for reflecting on this process. We 'soak up' ideas and inspirations until we reach saturation, take a break, discuss, debate and wait until the sponge dries again to restart the whole process.]

[Talking about his work as a composer, John Cage (in Iddon, 2019, p. 239) explains: "Composing's one thing, performing's another, listening's a third. What can they have to do with one another?" When communicating around interculturality, let's always bear in mind that we take part in different processes, which may or may not intersect. What I write about, say, listen to and negotiate with others in-/directly might not meet. It is thus important to find ways of bridging these different outlets of communication to reshape interculturality again and again, and to restart new conversations.]

[Translation of data and quotes doesn't just serve the purpose of decorating our publications on interculturality, but they are meant to contribute to both communication with and stimulation of our readers. Every time we translate, we need to think about the concrete person we are involving. How much are we respecting their 'original' voice? How can we make their voice more 'animated'? How can we share our hesitations as to how and what they speak of? Translation is always a 'work in progress' (like interculturality). It can never be ready but always in-between. Translation in communicating around interculturality is thus always *failess* – a new word containing hints of failure and success (on neoliberalism and the obsession/limits of success, see Clack & Paule, 2018).]

[We should accept that not everything can be translated or that it should be retranslated again and again. As a consequence, for, e.g., research, things should be re-analyzed and re-interpreted *with* others.]

[Exploring the (endless) process of translation could include:

- Going back to old translations of ours and others' and checking how fair they are to others' voices;
- Observing data analysis against the translations a given document contains and how they might mislead the reader;
- Being sensitive to 'hints' of translation in what we review, teach, supervise, co-write and co-collect data;
- For a day, noting down all decisions we make in relation to translation for and with interculturality.]

[All scholars and educators should experience being translated, confronting their own voice by their own voice being projected by someone else. As scholars and educators, we constantly include, express (and even fantasize) others' voices.]

[We should create new words whenever we have reached the impossibility of communicating: neologisms, portmanteau words or imported words from other languages. These should all be considered as temporary solutions, *mere Band-Aids*.]

[Reflexive and critical potpourri]

- As we are reaching the end of this book, what do you make of this statement: "language for communicating around interculturality can be an *impasse* although it might appear as a *passe-partout*"?
- How concerned are you by the phenomenon of 'academic tribes'? How much does it affect communicating around interculturality in research and education?
- Explore each of my 'remices' and reflect on how you position yourself in relation to the issues described in them. Which of my 'remices' would you reject or add to and why?
- The Chinese saying introduced by one of the students in the chapter could also guide us in communicating around interculturality: "忠言逆耳利于行" (in English: *a salutary diatribe* – 'hard words break no bones'). Reflect on how this could occur between us in ways that contribute to co-constructing new knowledge(s) together.
- For a day, observe the kinds of translational processes that you go through in your private and professional lives, translating sub-/consciously from and to other languages, dialects, sociolects . . . Reflect on your observations (what, where, who with, why . . .).
- Finally, do you also believe that 'slowing down' in the way we (are pushed to) communicate around interculturality could be beneficial for the world? Why (not)?

[Recommended reading]

May, S., & Caldas, B. (Eds.). (2022). *Critical ethnography, language, race/ism and education*. Multilingual Matters.

This edited book can help us explore further and enrich our take on communicating around interculturality – note that the authors centre mostly on the North American context. Although the chapters have to do with how students are themselves racialized and positioned as multilingual individuals, I believe that we can apply the form of critical ethnographic work presented by the authors to academics and scholars. As such, the book could nurture and galvanize our critical reflexivity in *critical and reflexive ways*.

Despagne, C. (2020). *Decolonizing language learning, decolonizing research: A critical ethnography study in a Mexican.* Routledge.

The focus of this book is on how (minority) students learn languages in postcolonial settings. Again, this is a bit far from what we do in research and education when communicating around interculturality, and yet, Despagne can inspire us to look at ourselves critically, infusing decolonial thinking and methods into what we utter, shout, suggest, impose and silence (as scholars and educators) beyond 'Westerncentric' ideologisms.

Shepherd, L. J. (2023). *The self, and other stories: Being, knowing, writing.* Rowman & Littlefield Publishers.

I am of the opinion that this important piece of auto-ethnographic reflection on the act of writing and the life of a researcher can nurture and galvanize our thinking about interculturality as an object of research and education. Shepherd interrogates her complex identities together with languaging of the world by scholars and teachers like herself (*being + knowing*), describing and exploring the pain academia has caused her. In so doing, she asks us to reimagine how knowledge production might differ if research was done and written about in other ways. Communicating around interculturality requires change and reimagining. Shepherd's book provides inspiration for making it happen.

Note

1 My translation of "Gary Magby a eu la sagesse, plutôt que de m'enseigner comme chanter une note, de m'apprendre comment laisser mon corps la chanter en paix et que ma voix ne soit pas entravée de pensées parasites. [. . .] Il me disait qu'il faut être en accord avec ta voiE pour comprendre ta voiX. Et c'est quelque chose qui revenait très, très souvent dans son cours, il me disait qu'il y a deux voix qui ne veulent pas toujours aller dans la même direction".

References

Barrett, M., & Golubeva, I. (2022). From intercultural communicative competence to intercultural citizenship: Preparing young people for citizenship in a culturally diverse democratic world. In T. McConachy, I. Golubeva, & M. Wagner (Eds.), *Intercultural learning in language education and beyond: Evolving concepts, perspectives and practices* (pp. 60–83). Multilingual Matters.

Becher, T. (2001). *Academic tribes and territories.* Open University Press.

Berger, J. (2008). *Ways of seeing.* Penguin.

Berheim, B. (2022). *La voix a des limites, la voie qui sait?* Interview. www.radiofrance.fr/franceculture/podcasts/affaires-culturelles/benjamin-bernheim-est-l-invite-d-affaires-culturelles-7251668

Boulez, P. (1986). *Orientations – collected writings.* Faber & Faber.

Camus, A. (2013). *Carnets* (Vol. 2). Folio.

Cioran, E. (1983). *Drawn and quartered.* Arcade Publishing.

Clack, B., & Paule, M. (Eds.). (2018). *Interrogating the neoliberal lifecycle: The limits of success.* Palgrave Macmillan.

Clarkson, A. (2005). A note on ". . . zwei Gefühle . . .", Musik mit Leonardo. *Contemporary Music Review, 24*(1), 53–55.

Danping, W. (2022). Translanguaging as a decolonising approach: Students' perspectives towards integrating Indigenous epistemology in language teaching. *Applied Linguistics Review*, OnlineFirst. https://www.degruyter.com/document/doi/10.1515/applirev-2022-0127/html

Dervin, F., & Chen, N. (2023). *Interculturality as an object of research and education: Observing, reflecting and critiquing.* Springer.

Dervin, F., & Tan, H. (2022). *Supercriticality and intercultural dialogue.* Springer.

Despagne, C. (2020). *Decolonizing language learning, decolonizing research: A critical ethnography study in a Mexican.* Routledge.

Genette, G. (1979). *Seuils.* Seuil.

Hanley, C. (2020). *George Orwell and education.* Routledge.

Holmes, P., Reynolds, J., & Ganassin, S. (2022). *The politics of researching multilingually.* Multilingual Matters.

Iddon, M. (2019). *John Cage and Peter Yates: Correspondence on music criticism and aesthetics.* Cambridge University Press.

Joppke, C. (2018). War of words: Interculturalism v. multiculturalism. *Comparative Migration Studies, 6,* Article 11.

Kaniskan, E. (2018). Kintsugi: Yara izlerinin güzelliği [Kintsugi, the beauty of wound scars]. *Ulakbilge Dergisi, 6*(21), 161–178.

Lachenmann, H. (1996). *Musik als existentielle Erfahrung.* Berlin: Breitkopf & Härtel.

May, S., & Caldas, B. (Eds.). (2022). *Critical ethnography, language, race/ism and education.* Multilingual Matters.

R'boul, H. (2022). Epistemological plurality in intercultural communication knowledge. *Journal of Multicultural Discourses, 17,* 173–188.

Shen, W., Xu, X., & Wang, X. (2022). Reconceptualising international academic mobility in the global knowledge system: Towards a new research agenda. *Higher Education, 84,* 1317–1342.

Shepherd, L. J. (2023). *The self, and other stories: Being, knowing, writing.* Rowman & Littlefield Publishers.

Victoria, M. (2022). *Methodological issues and challenges in researching transculturally.* Cambridge Scholars Publishing.

Von der Ruhr, M. (2006). *Simone Weil.* Continuum.

5 Communicating as a lesson in humility

[Vocalizing]

1. Go back to your notes from the previous chapters and summarize three takeaways about communicating around interculturality in research and education.
2. Communicating around interculturality involves negotiating economic-political agendas and ideologies, which can often be hidden behind 'beautified' discourses and words. Can you recall having engaged with someone around interculturality whose *camouflaged intentions* you managed to discover?
3. What are your views now on the simplistic dichotomy of the 'good' and 'bad' communicator in relation to how interculturality can be conceptualized and problematized?

During the months I was working on this book, I became increasingly aware of the fact that I was constantly experiencing what I was trying to describe and problematize in the previous chapters, as a scholar and an educator but also as a friend, a partner and a 'citizen' of this world. This morning, for instance, I was talking to my Chinese curator online. For his latest exhibition, we spent a lot of time negotiating and re-translating the texts he had written for it. We struggled with translating the Chinese title of the exhibition, and after multiple proposals, trials, errors and ample discussions around the messages behind his art, we chose a title in English which, at first, seemed 'galaxies away' from the Chinese one. However, the essence of what my curator wanted to say through this specific art exhibition was 'perfectly' described by the English title, *'otherwise'*. During our conversation this morning, he mentioned that one visitor had been puzzled by the apparent 'mismatch' between the Chinese and English titles and had complained, laughing, that there was an 'error' in the translation. The curator then explained how he wanted the two titles to refer to the 'atmosphere' of the assembled art pieces, *differently-similarly*, in two very different languages. He also referred to Cassin's (2014) view that the process of translation, 'navigating' between languages, is an important reminder that we are not 'alone' in this world and that there are many other ways of expressing the same ideas in different corners of the world (and even close to 'home', sometimes closer than we think). He argued that we had not chosen an English title for 'Chinese audiences' (*only*) who would find a perfect match between the Chinese title and the English one, but for the 'world' . . . He felt however that the visitor was not too convinced. He continued using the word 'error' in Chinese, and even produced a 'dictionary' translation of the title in English found online.

I have often faced similar reticence in communicating around interculturality with colleagues from around the world. *You cannot use the word* ethnicity. *A form of intercultural education that includes the idea of race is unacceptable. You cannot translate the Chinese word* Minzu *by retaining the pinyin version of the Chinese characters; you must say* nationality. Similarly, *you should not use Hofstede; he is a culturalist*, or *I am surprised that the author does not include an important article by Byram in his list of references*. These are all strong assertions and orders that can easily short-circuit communication.

[A 'good' communicator is not someone who knows *how to communicate*, who can impose their thoughts *'convincingly'* or (even worse) *'successfully'*, but someone who constantly learns and tries out other ways of communicating *with* others (silence and accepting 'defeat' included) to expand both the content and format of their own contributions to global knowledge. A 'good' communicator 'does' humility.]

To me, the exhibition episode summarizes well what this book is about and what communicating around an object (in this book: interculturality) entails. Thinking about translation, which is at the core somehow of most of the discussions in the previous chapters, and thus about how to communicate around interculturality in different languages is a lesson in *humility* – we must accept that we can never reach perfection in these complex processes. For Ricoeur (2006, p. 33), mourning the impossibility of *absolute translation* leads to a renewed and modest form of communicating. Forcing readers, ourselves included, to step out of our/their languaging comfort zone is a central object in learning how to communicate together around interculturality – beyond, e.g., the idea of 'errors' as rehearsed by the exhibition visitor above. Following Samoyault (2021), I would tend to agree that "[for me] the practice of translation resembles fans that open one after the other and also tracks that close, like so many hypotheses, some better than others at certain times because we want to show something that we have not seen before".[1] Working through these opening fans seems to me like a good metaphor for what we could do as 'apprentice-translators-communicators' in intercultural research and education, who can never be fully ready for this daunting task – regardless of their seniority, fame . . .

[We need to take the use of different languages into account seriously when dialoguing around interculturality. Sloppy, uncritical and simplistic (views on) translation *do-/es* damage intercultural encounters, and there is a need to address this crucial problem and take the time to unpack the words that we use to (try to) talk to each other. Moving forward without ensuring 'good' understanding is equivalent to the absence of communication.]

I spend most days by myself, reading, writing and communicating online with students and colleagues. At times, I don't even use my (biological) voice for days. A friend of mine noted that I speak a lot when we are together *face-to-face* (she is one of the rare individuals I meet *physically*). Over the past three years, I have published a lot, feeling the urge to speak about the catastrophes that our world is experiencing through my production on interculturality. In other words: *I communicate (silently) a lot.*

My language skills are located within the Indo-European and Finno-Ugric spheres, which means that I need to resort to English, French and/or German as lingua francas to speak to people from outside my 'corner' of the world. Not knowing, e.g., Chinese, Swahili or Tagalog limits my epistemic and ideological world. Although my use of, e.g., English as a Global Language might appear to be some kind of a blessing, allowing me to talk to millions of people, careless engagement in the language often leads to mis- and non-understanding/-communicating. As I have mentioned repeatedly in my books and lectures (Dervin & Yuan, 2021), for example, translating Minzu as *ethnic* or *national* is not helpful in communicating with people from other parts of the world since this will bring to mind different kinds of images and ideological positions associated with the two English words, which will not translate the complex position of Minzu in Chinese society and history. Although I speak (silently) and communicate *a lot*, I am, in fact, linguistically unable to speak, write, read and listen to billions of people around the world – which cannot but limit my understanding, problematization and experiences of interculturality. *I am not the only scholar and educator in this situation.*

I do believe that we need to be realistic as individuals in terms of who we can reach out to and engage with interculturally. As a scholar from Finland, my range of interlocutors is, in fact, very limited. As such, I interact with *some* colleagues from the 'West', colleagues from *some* parts of China, *some* students from China and *some* parts of Europe. On a daily basis, I communicate with *some* people from the general public from different parts of the world. I tend to be in contact with *some* scholars who agree with me, who also have some interest in China and who share similar ideological positions on issues of interculturality. My interaction with, e.g., decision-makers, journalists and businessmen is nearly non-existent since I feel that I don't know how to communicate deeply with them. Our objectives and 'stakes' often differ. For example, over the past three years, some journalists from different countries have contacted me for interviews. However, I have systematically rejected their invitations to speak since 1. The 'speaking' formats are always too limited to express one's ideas in sophisticated ways and 2. The expectations often seem to be too (obviously) ideologically oriented – the range of *voices* too limited.

This is why I consider working with students and educators from as many different parts of the world as possible, engaging *honestly* (humility!) and *modestly* with scholars who are ready to (really) cooperate academically, challenging each other to move forward in the be process to be the most meaningful tasks today. Small changes observed in myself and in others during these interactions give me hope.

Taking things for granted in research and education, e.g., not expecting to have to change our opinions, ideological worlds and ways of speaking in front of and with others are all acts of *anti-interculturality*.

The book chapters have both problematized communicating around interculturality ((un-)voicing, scrutinizing) and provided some advice as to how one can nurture and galvanize what we 'do' and say together. Although my visions and critiques might have sounded somewhat pessimistic in the book, I consider 'lifelong' and 'constant' work on interculturality to be exciting and stimulating endeavours. I believe in preparing individuals to meet each other *endlessly*, without giving them the illusion that they will be 'perfect' at communicating around interculturality with others since there are so many aspects of their encounters that they cannot 'control' – language being the main issue. Providing them with theoretical and methodological tools to be self-reflective and self-critical (recognizing, e.g., the ideologies that pervade what they say); curious observers and listeners; modest and honest describers of what they believed in as members of (a) given society/-ies should be a priority in academia and education. Learning to be silent and to refrain from speaking over and for other people is also an essential skill to communicate *interculturally*, which we must all practice in times like ours where calls for, e.g., decoloniality and epistemic justice are heard increasingly (Ferri, 2023; R'boul, 2023).

[Reflexive and critical potpourri]

For this last Potpourri, I have collected some of my assertions and arguments from the different chapters. Reviewing each of them, reflect on your own (changing) positions towards the content of these quotes, bearing in mind your own experiences of communicating around interculturality. Consider them as what I see as the main takeaways of this book.

- Look at the state of the world in spring 2023: *interculturality is failing us*. What if the reasons for this failure are not because we haven't learnt each other's culture, become non-essentialists or adopted polysemic (and politically-manipulated) ideologies such as *tolerance* and *respect* but because we haven't been concentrating enough on how to communicate

around the notion in ways that have allowed us to change together, to reconsider the notion under newly negotiated perspectives or to adapt new forms of discourse around the notion that reflect criticality (of criticality), reflexivity and humility?
- 'Languaging' is constant in our neoliberal worlds, where one is urged to communicate as often as one can, even when one has nothing to say. In this constant flow and flood of words, communicating around interculturality in research and education represents an important objective, which could help shift and push self and others to other spaces of co-creation.
- A good communicator around interculturality should be a good listener first and foremost, someone who can pause, be silent and work with and against languaging.
- Are my own words about interculturality *ever* mine?
- We must discover ourselves anew in each act of communication concerning interculturality as an object of research and education. We must accept clashes within self and between self and others in the process – clashes that we can address at moment x, moment y or never. A small change in our ways of speaking and listening is a victory for interculturality.
- A simple look at a list of references used in a book/an article (which indicates acts of communication in the process of writing somehow) can reveal how ideologies and capitalism are distributed and dominate the kind of communication that an author wishes to project. What languages are included? Which economic-political contexts? Whose dominating/marginal voices? What silences? Etc.
- We must care about translation as much as we care about (randomly) 'culture', 'identity', 'rationality', 'post-. . .', 'ethics', 'social justice' . . . as interculturalists. We must include it, problematize it, renegotiate and revise it; we must admit to its failures and successes. Translation should not just be a mere footnote in research papers and books.
- Any form of intercultural training always relies on 'indoctrination' one way or another. What I mean is: the way we scholars and educators teach (about) interculturality is always *political – we pass on ideologies, beliefs and certainties for a notion that should not be considered under such lenses*. This always relates to the way we see 'self', 'other', 'society', 'community', etc. and the way we talk about them.
- The *inter-* of interculturality concerns the scholar too and especially the scholar commenting on the other . . . who is at their mercy.

Note

1 My translation of "Pour moi, la pratique de la traduction, ce sont des éventails qui s'ouvrent les uns après les autres et aussi des pistes qui se ferment, comme autant d'hypothèses, certaines meilleures que d'autres à certains moments parce qu'on veut faire voir quelque chose qu'on n'a pas vu jusqu'alors".

References

Cassin, B. (Ed.). (2014). *Philosopher en langues: Les intraduisibles en traduction*. Editions Rue d'Ulm.

Dervin, F., & Yuan, M. (2021). *Revitalizing interculturality in education*. Routledge.

Ferri, G. (2023). Embodied others and the ethics of difference: Deterritorialising intercultural learning. *Pedagogy, Culture & Society, 31*(2), 269–282.

R'boul, H. (2023). Intercultivism and alternative knowledges in intercultural education. *Globalisation, Societies and Education*, OnlineFirst, 1–13.

Ricoeur, P. (2006). *On translation*. Routledge.

Samoyault, T. (2021). *Tiphaine Samoyault: "Aucune traduction n'est définitive, toutes les traductions doivent être refaites"*. Interview. www.radiofrance.fr/franceculture/podcasts/les-nuits-de-france-culture/la-nuit-de-la-traduction-entretien-3-3-avec-tiphaine-samoyault-1ere-diffusion-03-10-2021-9350727

Index

aboriginal 18
academic tribes 67, 81
AI 46, 52
alienation 3, 46
anti-racism 5, 46, 50
anxiety 27, 76
archeology 19, 22
audiobiography 32

balancing 8, 37, 54, 62, 72
borrowing 17, 40, 56, 69
brainwashing 9, 38, 77
burning issues 1

calligraphy 18–19
camouflage 21, 43, 84
cannibal capitalism 40, 55
certainties 71, 76, 88
China 3–6, 18–19, 32, 52, 56, 59–60, 69, 71, 73–75, 86
Chinese 3–4, 6, 32, 37–38, 44, 48–50, 53, 55, 59, 61, 63, 69–70, 72–75, 78, 81, 84–86
civilization 3, 17, 55–56
comfort zones 11, 66, 76, 85
community 2, 18, 21, 43, 71, 88
conducting 1–2, 12, 25, 78
conformism 77
connotations 8, 17, 36, 46, 49, 54, 57, 60–61, 68, 78
consumers 7, 27, 53
contradictions 5, 11, 39, 43, 45, 71, 76–77
Council of Europe 41, 58, 70
COVID-19 3, 5, 30, 49
criticality 6–7, 12, 58, 77, 88
cultural confidence 3
culturally responsive 4–5, 69

debate 7, 15, 39, 45, 80
decision-makers 2, 7, 15, 57, 86
decolonizing 8, 18, 22, 29–30, 58, 67, 87
democracy 3, 42, 75
democratic culture 5, 20, 23, 30, 32, 44, 58, 71
dialogism 20
dialogue 3, 20, 29, 33, 41, 67, 78
dictionary 16, 46, 49, 55, 85
discomfort 73
disseminate 18, 22, 36, 63
diversity 41, 50, 59, 69, 75
dominating 4–5, 10, 18, 20, 30–31, 40–42, 44, 46, 58, 66, 68–69, 88
Doxa 24, 47

economic 3, 9, 23, 40, 42, 44, 50, 54, 58, 68, 70–71, 78, 88
educators 2–5, 7, 9–10, 18, 20, 24, 27, 32, 36, 40, 42, 46, 52–53, 56, 57–59, 71, 76, 81–82, 84, 87–88
Englishes 54, 61
English as a Lingua Franca 52, 59
enslave 43, 45
epistemic justice 87
error 84–85
ethics 2–3, 23, 40, 50, 52, 72, 88
ethnocentric 30, 38
euro-centric 53, 62
European Union 5, 41

face-to-face 13, 30, 40, 94
fetishizing 76
Finland 1, 5, 29–30, 32, 59, 75–77, 86
Finnish 17, 52, 54, 66
flavours 52–53
flow and flood of words 7, 27, 33, 88

fragments 11, 23, 27, 31, 52, 80
French 16, 20, 33, 37, 46, 51, 55, 61, 68, 78, 86

Gamelan 24–25
general public 2, 86
genres 7, 11
Global South 18, 67

humility 6, 60, 68, 84–89

ideologemes 38, 40, 42, 44, 68
ideological clash 44, 72
ideological silos 9, 67
ideology 5–6, 9–10, 20–23, 30–32, 36–45, 47, 54, 62–63, 67–71, 75–77, 79, 84, 87–88
imperfections 57, 78
inclusion 11, 21–22, 32, 41, 53, 69, 72–73, 78, 81, 85, 88
incompleteness 21, 77–78
inconsistencies 5, 76
indoctrination 9, 68, 71, 76–77, 88
intercultural citizenship 23, 50, 69
intercultural competence 20, 37, 44, 58, 61, 79
interculturalists 2–4, 10–11, 33, 51, 53–54, 58–60, 62, 88
interculturalize 54, 58
internationalization 47, 59

languaging 7, 45–46, 48–50, 54, 60, 66, 72, 79, 82, 85, 88
legitimacy 47
lies 11, 23, 77
listening 7, 11, 13, 18, 27, 30, 42, 45, 57, 70, 75, 79–80, 88
list of references 42, 85, 88

marginal 42, 88
media 3, 26, 28, 30, 38, 47, 49, 59, 61
metaphor 12, 25, 80, 85
Minzu 4, 6, 32, 44, 69–71, 85–86
misquote 21
misunderstanding 3, 8, 20–21, 37, 75
money 22, 41, 45, 55
multicultural 4, 10, 41, 44, 49, 69–70, 73
multilingual 8, 22, 49–50, 52, 57, 70
music 1–2, 15–16, 24–25, 27, 29, 31, 53
music conductor 1, 2, 12, 25

nationalism 38, 63
neoliberal 7, 30, 50, 80, 88
neologism 45, 81
non-essentialism 6, 39, 41, 43, 87

obsession 5, 33, 80
OECD 41, 70
orders 20, 21, 42, 57, 75, 77, 85
orthodoxy 24, 42

paratexts 73
passe-partout 36–37, 66, 81
philosophy 8, 45, 75
policies 4, 12, 55
political 3, 6, 9, 18, 23, 29, 38, 40, 42, 44, 52, 54–55, 57–59, 68–72, 88
polysemic 4, 6, 10, 22, 37–38, 43, 48, 57, 70, 76, 87
privilege 18, 30, 42, 67, 70
producers 7, 79
promoters 3, 6–7, 75, 79

race 22, 46, 69–71, 74, 78, 81, 85
racism 5, 46, 50
readers 4–5, 8, 11–13, 28, 37, 49–50, 54–58, 71–72, 80, 85
reflexivity 2–3, 6, 11–12, 26, 39, 49, 57–59, 62, 73, 81, 87–88

silence 30–32, 37–38, 42–43, 66, 88
silencing 9, 23, 29–30, 68, 70
slogans 12
slowing down 78, 81
social justice 43, 53, 58, 88
speaking over 67, 87
stereotypes 9, 28, 32, 39, 40, 44, 47, 62, 71
subjectivities 9–10, 66

teachers 6–7, 15–16, 32, 38, 59, 71–72, 82
technique 2, 16, 25
throwing voices 15–16
tolerance 3, 6, 30, 42, 71, 74, 87
tongues 45
translators 50–51, 53, 56, 58–62, 85

untranslatable 72

walls 78
West (The) 3, 18, 20, 28, 30, 70, 74–75, 86
Western-centric 41, 70, 79, 82

For Product Safety Concerns and Information please contact our EU representative GPSR@taylorandfrancis.com
Taylor & Francis Verlag GmbH, Kaufingerstraße 24, 80331 München, Germany

www.ingramcontent.com/pod-product-compliance
Lightning Source LLC
Chambersburg PA
CBHW051758230426
43670CB00012B/2346